CW01064851

Shakespeare's Mentor

Anthony R. Munday

Copyright © 2017 Anthony R. Munday

All rights reserved, including the right to reproduce this book, or portions thereof in any form. No part of this text may be reproduced, transmitted, downloaded, decompiled, reverse engineered, or stored, in any form or introduced into any information storage and retrieval system, in any form or by any means, whether electronic or mechanical without the express written permission of the author.

The views expressed in this work are solely those of the author and do not necessarily reflect the views of the publisher, and the publisher hereby disclaims any responsibility for them.

ISBN: 978-1-365-80385-7

PublishNation
www.publishnation.co.uk

For Margaret

1946 – 2018

Contents

Introduction

The life of William Shakespeare in London is unknown. Shakespeare, the man, does not appear in Elizabethan London's historical records. The plays and poems were produced in London, but he, the person, cannot be found. Most of his contemporary writers do appear in London's historical records; yet he, the most famous of them all, is missing. There has to be a rational explanation for this lack of any records of his socialising or interacting with contemporaries.

The life of William Shakspere in Stratford-upon-Avon is known of in some detail. Researchers, over many years, have studied his life in Stratford in depth and found many events in his life there. When he was born, who his family were, who he married and when his children were born. Their various homes and when and where he died. His vast wealth and final family home in Stratford-upon-Avon, New Place, are well known. Even purchases and court cases where he sued or was sued over some matter have been uncovered. His five varied signatures and differing spellings of his surname have also been found in Stratford. Some books then attempt to construct a life in London through his plays and poems. The reason for this is, as stated above, that there are no records of him in London. This has skewed the telling of the history of London Shakespeare. Analysing the written works attributed to Shakespeare is the only source of information. A great deal of what is said is confirmation bias. An example of this is the claim that he must have attended Stratford Grammar School, simply because the stories include too much knowledge for him not to have done so. The possibility that he had help in writing and plotting is not considered. Another example is that he must have visited Italy, because of the detailed knowledge of it in the plays. If he himself had never been there –and it is almost certain that he had not– then it points to him having a friend that did know Italy very well. There has to be a good reason why Shakespeare, in London, is invisible; there is something important missing from his life story. Thus, I am convinced that other authors were involved in many of Shakespeare's works. The Two Noble Kinsmen, written by William Shakespeare and John Fletcher, is not the only play co-written. This being so, why does no one ever mention meeting him? An important dimension of his life, his circa twenty-five years living in London, is missing from the accepted story.

The logical resolution to this mystery is that he was never an author in London at all, and thus, London's William Shakespeare was actually someone's pen name. It is tempting to believe this and today a great many people are convinced that it is the truth. This factual book begins with a unique view of the authorship problem. This view is that Stratford-Shakespeare was, or became, a shy recluse who avoided social interactions and gatherings. Thus, he would only be happy in the company of one or two literary friends. If this theory is a true reflection of his life in London, then it follows that someone had to be in charge of his literary affairs and act as his business manager. There is no direct evidence that anyone did take on that role. No name comes up strongly within his known life, and no one hinted or claimed to be that person. None-the-less, if this manager existed, then he must have left a trail.

There is one prolific writer of the times whose life and works do continually merge with London-Shakespeare's literary record. If Stratford-Shakespeare was also London-Shakespeare, then he must have had a mentor cum manager in London, and this must be that man.

Late 1500s London

William Shakspere was born in Stratford-upon-Avon in April 1564. He grew up there and married Anne Hathaway. They had three children, Susanna in 1583, then twins Hamnet and Judith in 1585. At some time after the birth of his twin children, he moved to London leaving his family behind. Other events suggest he left his family to seek his fortune in literate endeavours around 1588.

Twenty-four-year-old was almost too late to suddenly have an all-embracing urge to leave his established life, to become a playwright. Then, at the same time, for him to also change into some form of a recluse is uncanny. There are, though, things that could have caused these changes. A blow to the head, a serious disease, or suffering prolonged mental or physical pain could be the cause of a personality shift. If the genius writer was stirred within him, it could never fully bloom in the cultural backwater of sixteenth-century Stratford-upon-Avon. He would have had to move to the centre of it all, London. This sudden lurch into literature could be the reason that he has left no handwritten, printed, or referenced literary records of his writings before moving to London. Nor any signatures on contracts or official documents.

In the year 1592, a didactic epistle titled "Groats-Worth of Witte" was printed. It is supposed to be a deathbed letter to the world by Robert Greene. In it, a playwright is criticised as being an upstart crow and referred to as *"in his conceit the only shake scene in a country"*. This is the first, generally accepted recorded allusion to the author William Shakspere in London. Shakspere is pronounced "shack-spur". The London spelling, "Shakespeare", was yet to appear. He was to spend almost half of his lifetime in London writing the plays and poems, but he never moved his family to live with him. It seems that the early plays were anonymous but then appeared in print with "Shakespeare" credited as the author. Unfortunately, this is all that is known about his life in London. There are no references to him, the person, at all. It seems he did not mix and did not socialise with his contemporary writers and artists. No one ever seems to have befriended him and written about him. No one mentions meeting him in London; not in a tavern, printers, church, theatre or the streets. No one wrote to him, and no one was written to by him. No one says they saw him act anywhere, and he did not contribute to The War of the Theatres, as it became known. This man, the most famous playwright in London, was not written about when he died in 1616. His name never appears in the Elizabethan treasure chest that is Philip Henslowe's theatrical diary of performances and payments.

The questions have to be considered; was he a recluse? Did he have a personality defect? Had he, therefore, a friend who acted as his guardian, mentor and business manager in London?

There is a man, well recorded in the Elizabethan–Jacobean period, who was one of the most prolific writers of the time. He also appears, to a remarkable degree, to have been a secret mentor to Shakespeare in London. This man was everywhere doing everything: Draper/printer, author, poet, actor, ballad writer, musician, singer, travel writer, journalist, playwright, polyglot, translator, government agent, Messenger to Her Majesties Chamber, pageant writer and producer, and literary executor of John Stow's Survey of London. This prolific genius was only three and a half years older than William Shakspere, but in printing, publication and playwrighting, he was a decade ahead. Shakspere could never equal him in detailed knowledge of printing and publication. But he could be taught the skills of writing for performance in London's new-concept theatres.

This factual book reveals the persistent links, and apparent coincidences, occurring during these two brilliant authors' parallel lives in London.

On the 13ᵗʰ of October 1560, a boy was baptised in St Gregory by St Paul's church in London. He was the son of Christopher and Jayne Munday and they named their son Anthony. Christopher was a draper but had changed trades to become a stationer. In those times a stationer was someone who published and printed books and pamphlets, as well as supplying paper, ink, etc. Anthony, therefore, grew up in a printing house. He thus had all the advantages that a printer's son could have. He became literate at an early age and would, no doubt, have easy access to plenty of expensive paper, ink and books. He read much and wrote much and became a child actor. He was first published in print at the age of sixteen years. It appears that he never stopped writing for the rest of his very long life.

Around the time of his eighteenth birthday in October 1578, he travelled to France and then Italy working for Queen Elizabeth's court. He landed in Boulogne and visited many cities including Amiens, Paris, Lyon, Milan, Bologna, Florence, Siena, Rome, Nice, Venice, Padua and Verona. He was still only eighteen-years-old when he arrived back in England in 1579. As well as acting and writing, he became a pursuivant, working for Richard Topcliffe under Sir Francis Walsingham. It seems that this loyalty to Queen Elizabeth was recognised and rewarded because he was appointed a Messenger of Her Majesties Chamber. This position required him to travel the length and breadth of the realm. As a further result of this work, he was also made Poet to the City of London. He married and had five children. His wife was Elizabeth, and their first child was named after her. Daughter Elizabeth was baptised on the 28 June 1584. She was followed by Rose on the 17 Oct 1585, but she died three months later. Priscilla was baptised on the 9 Jan 1587, followed by their only son, Richard, on the 27 Jan 1588. Their last child was Anne, baptised on the 5 Sept 1589.

The body of written work Munday produced was astounding and his name makes many appearances in Philip Henslowe's theatrical diary. At some time, long after his death and probably in the 1800s, he began to be referred to as a hack writer or lesser playwright. Considering what is recorded in his name, these epithets do not make sense. None-the-less, they seem to have stuck. Munday was attacked during his lifetime by other playwrights but he was not alone in this. There were several groupings having a pop at each other, and it seems it was as much about publicity as disdain. To quote Oscar Wilde:
"There is only one thing worse than being talked about, and that is not being talked about".

Even Shakespeare was attacked in this way, as the Parnassus plays show us. [discussed later]

Anthony Munday had an association with Edward de Vere, the Earl of Oxford. He became his servant (secretary) for some time and dedicated some of his works to him. He, it is believed, was one of the prompts that convinced Munday to travel to France and Italy. Although he returned to England in 1579, he did not publish his book about the journey, The English Roman Life, until 1582. The assumption is, that because it reported details of insults and threats against Queen Elizabeth and her Protestant rule, it was spiked for a while. It is possible that the delay was also because the names of the quoted people were recorded. So those people the book obliquely identified, who were at that time still living abroad, were not made aware that they were under investigation by publishing the book too soon. Munday's detailed knowledge of Italy is confirmed in this book. The story about his tour of France and Italy is briefly as follows.

Munday set out for France in about November 1578 with a companion, Thomas Nowell. They were instructed to find out about the colleges that were training priests to send into England and to confirm that the famous Douai college had moved to Reims. Their first planned stop was to find an English Catholic priest in Amiens, who could recommend them to study in the, newly relocated, English College at Reims. Before they got to Amiens they were robbed on the road and left destitute. Having then, later, located the priest and asked for help, they convinced him that they were sympathetic to Catholicism. The priest, probably to get them off his patch and out of his purse, gave them a few coins and a letter of introduction to the Reims College. In addition, they were also entrusted to deliver a separate letter to the rector, Dr Allen, in Reims. Having obtained this written confirmation that the Douai College had, indeed, re-located to Reims, they instead went to Paris to find the English Ambassador, Sir Amias Paulet. They delivered the letters to him. They must have met Francis Bacon, who was the Ambassador's assistant at that time. Munday and Nowell were eighteen-year-old youths and Bacon almost eighteen years, so all three are likely to have associated together for the few days that Munday and Nowell enjoyed in Paris. Although Bacon was there, he is not mentioned or referred to in Munday's book. I believe Bacon and Munday had a lifelong literary friendship after their Parisian junket. If Munday was Shakespeare's mentor, this could have led to the connection some people see between Shakespeare's and Bacon's writings.

During that week in Paris, Munday and Nowell, pretending to sympathise with Catholicism, met many self-exiled English Catholic gentlemen. Speculation about who he was, led to Munday acquiring the alias of Anthony Hawley. He used this alias until he returned to England the following year. Those English gentlemen, by entertaining Munday and Nowell, got to know them well. They then procured them letters of introduction and persuaded both men to travel to Rome to join the English College there. In Rome, both men became seminary priests, and they spent many weeks studying the priesthood. Munday, in his much-delayed book, The English Roman Life, tells of the sightseeing tours around Rome; about the Churches and relics and the three-day Carne Vale celebrations. Then he reveals the confrontational problems between the Welsh and English seminary priests, and the subsequent appeals to Cardinal Morone, for fair play. After many failed meetings, the English seminaries threatened to leave Rome and were summoned to an audience with Pope Gregory XIII. This was the Pope who, subsequently, introduced the Gregorian calendar. The Pope listened to their complaints and ruled in their favour, so all went well for a short while. When it became time to take the oath to become Catholic priests, Munday dodged it. He left the seminary in Rome and toured Italy. He visited Nice, Venice, Padua, Verona, and many other cities, before retracing his steps back through France to the channel ports and home.

The knowledge of France and Italy that Munday gained from his tour was vast. So, if Munday did later have an association with Shakespeare, he would be the unexplained source of knowledge about Italy, which Shakespeare later wrote so much about in the plays.

In 1580 Anthony Munday wrote a book with the very long title of:
"Zelauto. The Fountain of Fame. Erected in an Orchard of Amorous Adventures. Containing a Delicate Disputation, gallantly discoursed between two noble Gentlemen of Italy."
By A.M. Servant to the Right Honourable the Earl of Oxford.

This book is usually referred to nowadays as "Zelauto: The Fountain of Fame". There is only one extant original copy and that is preserved in the Bodleian Library in Oxford. It has been photographically copied and can be bought as originally printed, but it is difficult to read as it is in a blackletter typeface and uses contractions in place of some syllables. The preferred choice is to source a copy edited by Jack Stillinger and published, initially, as a limited edition of 1500 copies in 1963. The copy numbers are to be found at the end of the book. At the time of writing, excellent copies of the 1963 limited edition become available regularly.

Jack Stillinger points out that this book by Munday is only the sixth, or possibly, even only the fifth Elizabethan novel to be published, and it is the first English novel to use chapter divisions. Munday created chapters or introduced them into English literature. He read many foreign books, he was a polyglot and had Latin, French and Italian. Plus, to some degree, Greek and Spanish, as well as his mother tongue; Elizabethan English. This seminal treasure of English literature, Zelauto, is almost universally ignored. Somewhat in the manner that the prolific and ubiquitous Anthony Munday, is usually missing from references to Elizabethan authorship.

Zelauto is the son of the governor of Venice and the story of his journey is in three parts, the last part contains the plot that reappears in Shakespeare's The Merchant of Venice sixteen years later.

Compare the following short extracts. From Munday's Zelauto–1580. Signor Truculento is giving evidence before a judge in Verona. Strabino and Rodolfo owe money to Truculento. They are defended by Cornelia and Brisana, their wives. Incidentally, two intelligent and strong women, something else of Munday's pressed into Shakespeare.

"The rendering of the money I do not account of, nor will I be pleased with twice as much restored: the breach of the Law I mean to exact and to use rigor where it is required. The forfeiture of their lands is the one part of the penalty. The loss of their right eyes the whole in general ..." then eight pages of pleas and defences and legal interventions before Cornelia asks for a ruling of the judge that Truculento:

"Under verdict of my Lord his licence. I give you in charge and also especially notifie, that no man but your self shall execute the deede, ne shall you crave any counsayle of any the standers by. If in pulling foorth their eyes, you diminise the least quantitie of blood out

of their heads, over and besided their only eyes, or spyll one dop in taking them out...”

From Shakespeare's The Merchant of Venice–1596. Shylock is giving evidence before a judge in Venice having refused twice what he is owed.

Shylock. "We trifle time: I pray thee pursue sentence."
Portia. "A pound of that same merchant's flesh is thine. The court awards it and the law doth give it."
Shylock. "Most rightful judge!"
Portia. "And you must cut this flesh from off his breast. The law allows it and the court awards it."
Shylock. "Most learned judge! A sentence! Come, prepare."
Portia. "Tarry a little, there is something else. This bond doth give thee here no jot of blood: The words expressly are'a pound of flesh ..."

These are the same stories and plots. If the story had been copied from Zelauto by Shakespeare, he would not have looked for predictable trouble from Munday and his business associates, by only moving the setting from Verona to the not-far-off city of Venice. Both cities are in the north of Italy, and they even begin with the same letter of the alphabet. If Munday was his mentor and working alongside him, then he will have been happy to help his friend with a good plot, and there would be no cause for any trouble between them.

It may be of interest to Americans, North and South, that Munday makes a passing mention of the continent on page 41 of Zelauto, "The golden American country".

In 1579, at the age of nineteen, Munday published The Mirror of Mutability. In the introduction to this book, Munday mentions some of the cities he visited when abroad. As the story of his Italian journey was yet to be published, this appears to be a marketing device by him to tempt his readers. This was then added to by another line in the introduction:

"I journeyed into Italy, to Rome, Naples, Venice, Padua, and diverse other excellent Cities."

Coming from Venice through Padua, means he visited Verona, as that is where the road leads to. He then adds:

"Yet my web of youthful time was not fully woven, and my wild oats required to be sowed in foreign ground."

Is he also promising romance in the forthcoming publication of The English Roman Life? If he was, he didn't deliver it in this book; but it does come out in the romantic Shakespeare play set in Verona. Did he tell Shakespeare more about his Italian journey? The name Romeo is, of course, from the city of Rome, where Munday had spent many weeks studying for the priesthood. Did he give Shakespeare another story?

I have a personal view that the first London-Shakespeare play, The Two Gentlemen of Verona, was written a lot earlier than the year 1589 given by E.K. Chambers. The Alexandra Text gives it as 1584, and that seems more accurate to me. This would mean that William Shakspere went to London after the birth of Suzzana in May 1583 but before the twin children were born in January 1585. There is a view that the first play was written even earlier, but that raises irreconcilable authorship problems for Stratford-Shakspere. Like it or not, this all seems to suggest that he deserted his family after the birth of the twins. He cannot have written forty plays in twenty-eight years, plus the poems and sonnets, and then spent much time in Stratford-upon-Avon. If we take Alexander's earlier date of 1584, that would be one play, fully finished, with him then acting in it, every thirty-six weeks, without a break, for twenty-eight years. With the Chamber's date, it would be even tighter. It is little wonder no one ever records meeting him in London. He never had time to go out.

Shakespeare must have been in London by 1588. There is a consensus (though disputed) that the first play was Two Gentlemen of Verona and that play shouts of Munday's input. The play is set in Italy and is basically a reversal of part of Munday's not-so-grand tour of France and Italy. The first fifty words of this play is a synopsis of the conversations Munday would have had before he went abroad.

ACT ONE
Scene 1. Verona. An open place.
Enter VALENTINE and PROTEUS.

Val.
Cease to persuade, my loving Proteus:
Home-keeping youth have ever homely wits.
Were't not affection chains thy tender days
To the sweet glances of the honour'd love,
I rather would entreat thy company
To see the wonders of the world abroad,
Than living dully sluggardiz'd at home,
Wear out thy youth with shapeless idleness.
But since thou lov'st, love still, and thrive therein,
Even as I would, when I to love begin.

The author is almost bragging about being adventurous and mocking his friend for being too comfortable at home *"dully sluggardiz'd "* and wasting his youth in *"shapeless idleness"*. This is a conversation Munday must have had several times prior to setting out on his continental tour when he was trying to persuade friends to accompany him.

Munday is not only advising Shakspere, but he is also writing alongside him. This means that if Shakspere wrote alone when he first moved to London, then he was in London a great deal earlier than 1588. Nothing of what he wrote before Two Gentlemen of Verona exists today. It has all vanished. This would suggest that Munday had a positive influence on Shakspere's writings. It was lifted up from being good stories to being good performances on the stage. Considering what a genius writer Shakspere was, that influence, as already speculated, was likely to have been in generating plots and adapting Shakspere's writings to theatre performances. The scenes, modern theatre props, continuity, timings and directions would all be new to Shakspere. He would have been in his early twenties and must have brought with him some of his previous writings. They have not survived in any form at all, neither in London nor in Stratford, so we can't judge what influence Munday had on him if he was his mentor.

9

Sometime before 1590, Anthony Munday wrote a comedy play titled "John a Kent and John a Cumber". Only his original handwritten copy is extant and bears the date of December 1590. The date was added to the manuscript and was not in Munday's autograph, so only indicates the play was written before then. No one knew of its existence until the mid-1800s, when it turned up in the possession of a gentleman from Wales. It was copied and first printed in 1851. The man entrusted with the publication of the play was John Payne Collier. He was a disreputable Shakespeare researcher and expert. It was, later in his life, discovered that he was a forger, who interfered with the historical record, in an effort to create proofs that Shakspere had been in London. He, too, was well aware of the conundrum of the dearth of London records mentioned above. Collier was also an expert on Anthony Munday, which, presumably, is why he was given the task of producing the first printing of Munday's play. He first praises, then criticises Munday in the forward to the book. He sees that this play has reflections in Shakespeare's, The Tempest, and this seems to bother him so much, that he feels he has to denigrate Munday. This opinion from a wrong'un may be the precursor of all the oft-repeated epithets, "hack" or "lesser playwright", which it seems is de-rigueur to include in any mention of Munday in literature today. I know of no one else from the times who has these insults welded to his reputation.

Personally, I am coming to view these historical put-downs as validations of achievement; nailing the atavistic grisly shock felt by Collier et al. when a visceral sensation informed them that this contemporary genius had a close association with William Shakespeare.

It would appear that logic and common sense never entered Collier's world to suggest that the two men could be connected in some way. This obfuscation was in spite of his knowing that these men were London contemporaries. They must have frequented the same theatres, publishers, stationers, churches, taverns and social groupings for many years. It is impossible that they were not together on many occasions. Collier should have realised that Munday was, at the very least, associating with Shakespeare. The possibility that Munday was, in fact, Shakespeare's manager and that this explained some of his, Collier's, London-Shakespeare problems, must have constantly stewed in his brain. Why did he reject his discovery?

The relevant quote from Collier about Munday's play, John a Kent and John a Cumber, is:

"...for he raises no fewer than four different preternatural agents, or Antics, for the purpose of misleading his adversary, John a Cumber, and those who trusted in him. These Antics sing four songs; and John a Kent's boy, Shrimp, who is a very useful coadjutor, possesses the faculty of becoming invisible, and, like Ariel in "The Tempest," by his magical music induces persons to follow him, until they lose their way, and lie down to sleep from weariness. In any other particulars we would not for an instant be supposed to institute a comparison between the most beautiful and delicate creation our poetry can boast, [Shakespeare] and the coarse and comparatively vulgar invention of a great, but far inferior dramatist. [Munday]

So, yes, he concedes that Shakespeare got this from Munday's play, but no credit at all must be leaked to the creator of the "vulgar invention".

Collier had been tasked with critiquing for publication Munday's, rediscovered, handwritten play. In doing this, he found a strong connection to Shakespeare. So, why did Collier feel compelled to denigrate the author of –what was at that time– a 260 years-old play? What was really in going on in his mind?

Content from John a Kent and John a Cumber is also in the Shakespeare play, The Merchant of Venice.

In 1598, Munday wrote his Robin Hood plays. The first was "The Downfall of Robert Earl of Huntington". Content from this play is found in Shakespeare's Othello.

The second Robin Hood play was "The Death of Robert Earl of Huntington". Content from this play is found in Shakespeare's Macbeth.

Both of these plays are set in forests. As You Like It, is also in a sylvan setting.

Much Ado About Nothing follows Munday's adaptation, Fedele and Fortunio, Two Italian Gentlemen. Munday adapted it from a Luigi Pasqualigo story.

So, what is going on here? There is nothing recorded about Munday challenging Shakespeare about this copying. Nor is there anything recorded about Shakespeare acknowledging Munday, or even that they were colleagues or friends. In fact, as Collier was well aware, nothing at all is recorded in London about William Shakespeare the person. The plays are recorded in London, but not him, the man. Could the simple resolution to this conundrum be that he was or became a shy recluse? Did Shakespeare have or develop a personality disorder where he hid away to avoid people? Can it be that the genius who wrote the works had a guardian-cum-mentor looking after him? He is supposed to have been an actor so this does not make complete sense. There is, however, the possibility that he only acted minor, spear-carrier parts. These parts would have no onerous duties; there would be no words to speak and little moving about the stage. Thus, it was the best position to be in to see how your new play went down with the audiences. Perhaps even this simple performance was difficult for him and he trembled a little, so began to shake the spear while looking out at the boisterous crowd. Could this be why his name changed? Perhaps it came about as a pun on his real name.

What is happening, though, is that Shakespeare is following Anthony Munday in his written works, and it is always Munday leading and Shakespeare following. There has to be a connection, so was Munday, Shakespeare's guardian in London and thus did all of his business negotiations? This could explain why Shakespeare is missing from London's literary record. If this is correct, then he is under Munday's management, and so, Anthony Munday must also have been his mentor in London.

If you read a book about the life of William Shakspere/Shakespeare, it will discuss only two things about him. The first is his life in Stratford-upon-Avon, and it will go into great detail about his family and the way of life in an Elizabethan country town. The second thing is the plays and poems. They will be discussed in great detail and at great length. What they are never able to discuss is the most important part of this man, the main things everyone would want to know; his famous life in London. His literary jousts with his contemporaries, his work in the theatres, the innovations he created, the important people he mixed with, his peccadillos, his indiscretions, his high points and low moods, the arguments and –as a man living separated from his family– the flirtations. All of these things are unknown and the reason, as explained above, is that there is nothing recorded about him. Without his London life, the man is hollowed out. Even the death of this famous London man from Stratford-upon-Avon is not recorded by anyone in London until seven years after he died. Even then, the First Folio of 36 plays tells us nothing about him, other than he passed away at some vague time in the past. It does not really even say that much; all it does is refer to him as already dead.

Could it be that William Shakspere was a reclusive savant who could only function as a genius under someone's protection? If this is true, Anthony Munday is the one man whose own life and works constantly link in with Shakespeare's. Many people knew of the famous man, Shakespeare, but in truth, he was someone that they never actually met, and knew nothing at all about, other than he wrote wonderful plays and poetry.

London Shakespeare

When William Shakspere first went to London, he must have been astounded by the performance of plays in the first, purpose-built, theatres. These were "The Theatre" and "The Curtain Theatre" in Shoreditch, London. Growing up in Stratford-upon-Avon, he would have only seen performances by strolling players. The performances would be in tavern yards and street corners and usually in stages. So, the first act would be performed in the morning, then the next act during the afternoon and act three the next morning, and so on. These were the original "stage plays" because they were performed in stages. The stories Shakspere would have seen would be old religious tales and some comedy tomfoolery. They would change little over the generations. Older people, having seen them time and again, would probably know them word for word. In London, watching and listening to a continuous complete performance, that you had never seen before, and on an elevated platform –which takes its name "stage" from the old stage plays– would be a technical wonder beyond imagination. It is reasonable to believe that Shakspere, initially, met someone in one of these theatres. It is likely that our reclusive, aspiring writer, remained back after a performance, probably gawking at the wonder of it all. As a new arrival in London, it would be the obvious thing for an aspiring playwright to do. A conversation with someone, possibly Munday, then showing his writings, may have been the catalyst for their future relationship. Munday could teach him something he did not know; how to convert a story into a play for performance in the new theatres. He would need to learn how to break it down so that a few actors could double up into different roles. Then, where to expand or delete sections for those actors to be able to change roles. Also, where to insert monologues to create time for major performance changes. After this, the reading to check that all of these changes still made sense as a story and that the continuity is maintained. Then he would need to create a short plot sheet, so all those involved would know what should be happening and when. Then the writing out of the various individual actors' characters' lines for them to learn, and to instruct them when they went on and came off. When all that was done, a prompt-book with all of the stage directions would have to be written up for the bookkeeper in charge to direct the performance. All of this preparation was newly developed for performances in the purpose-built London theatres. It was a great deal of extra work after the original story was written. The man who looked after and managed all of this work was called the bookkeeper because that is what he did; organise, proofread and keep the books of plays safe. Shakspere, when first in London, would be utterly lost in the new theatres. He would have had to become a stagehand cum spear-carrier at first, in order to eventually get his feet under the playwrights' table.

The first written record in London alluding to the name Shakespeare, is claimed to be in Robert Greene's, "Groats-worth of Witte". It is in three sections and was printed shortly after Greene's death in 1592. Some theatrical people are insulted by Greene in this publication. The words that Greene –or rather, Henry Chettle– actually use to describe the main person targeted by this, is "an upstart Crow", "Tiger's heart" and "Johannes factotum". The relevant quote is:

"Yes, trust them not: for there is an upstart Crow, beautified with our feathers, that with his Tiger's heart wrapped in a Players hide, supposes he is well able to bombast out a blank verse as the best of you: and being an absolute Johannes fac totum, is in his conceit the only Shake-scene in a country."

"Tiger's heart wrapped in a Players hide" is a paraphrase of *"O tiger's heart wrapp'd in a woman's hide!"* from Henry VI part three. There is, therefore, the belief that *"Shake-scene"*, somehow, refers to the author of the Shake-speare plays. It, though, does not mention plays, it refers to a *Player*, an actor. *"Bombast"* refers to pompous speech, not writing.

The words *Johannes fac totum* mean Jack of all trades in English. This points to someone who was involved in other employment. It does not make sense for it to be a criticism of Shakspere.

15

The book is supposed to be Greene's deathbed letter to the world. Greene, however, did not publish it. Henry Chettle published it, claiming it was all Greene's words and none of his. The copy given to the printers was all in Chettle's handwriting. The note in the printer's register reads *"upon the peril of Henry Chettle"*. So, it seems there were questions about its authorship from the very beginning.

Part two of Groatsworth is where the famous "Shake-scene" quote comes from. In this part, Greene first insults two people. The first one is, almost certainly, Christopher Marlowe. The insult about following in his, Greene's, sinful footsteps is nothing much to be bothered about, but Greene also says that Marlowe denied God, and this endangered Marlowe. It was an offence not to be a churchgoing Protestant at that time, let alone being an atheist.

The second person is described as "young junival" [Junival was a satirical Roman poet] and most people believe this person to be Thomas Nashe. None of the insults against Nashe is more than 'cease doing as I have done'.

Greene then greatly insults a third person. He is, *"upstart Crow"*, *"Tiger's heart"* and *"in his conceit the only Shake-scene in a country"*. There is a theory, that I support, that the Upstart Crow in Groats-worth of Witte, is referring to Edward Alleyn, a star actor of the times. He was a large man and it can be easily imagined, that when delivering a strong and emotional monologue, he would pace up and down the stage with heavy paces that would rattle the boards. The line; *"O tiger' heart wrapped in a woman's hide!"*, is from Henry VI part three. This line ends with an exclamation mark/point and occurs in a 39-line monologue. It was one of Alleyn's, Shake-scene monologues. Shake, as in shaking the stage. Shake-scene means exactly what it says.

There is no record of the name, Shakespeare, appearing on any printed works at this time. The name must have been well known but had not yet appeared in print. Handwritten copies of the plays would be used in the theatres and, presumably, well taken care of.

It is recorded that Edward Alleyn planned to build a windmill. The building of a windmill is referenced in the first part of Groats-worth. It is part of a discussion between Roberto (Greene) and a player (Alleyn). The player has heard Roberto muttering while resting behind a hedge. He is penniless and complaining about his poverty. The player offers him work writing plays for him and adds that he will be well paid. It seems to be a description of Greene and Alleyn's first meeting some years previously. It would have taken place in a tavern, rather than in the ditch/gutter alluded to.

Alleyn had now written a play of his own and this, it is thought, is partly what Greene is complaining about in Groatsworth. To Greene, Alleyn's play contained mirrors of his writings, therefore, it was not an original creation. This is the *"Johannes fac totum"* jibe. Alleyn was also the *"upstart crow, beautified with our feathers"*. So, made famous by performing the plays of professional writers and now plagiarising their knowledge. *"feathers"*, thus, quill pens.

Henry Chettle, in a later publication, says it was all Greene's words and none of his, but he added that he removed one thing that was too insulting to include.

Greene's Groats-worth of Witte is a long mea-culpa for his, Greene's, life of selfishness. Wine, women and the abandonment of his wife and child abroad. He knew he was dying and it seems was putting his affairs in order. Then, also, polishing up his reputation for posterity by repenting. His main complaint is about being abandoned by his friends, Edward Alleyn being one of them. This abandonment is reiterated in the Aesop tale of the ant and the grasshopper, which forms part three of Groats-worth. The story is that Ant and Grasshopper walk about the same green. Ant, all through the summer, gathers food for winter. The skipping Grasshopper doesn't and scorns Ant for needless thrift. When a bad winter comes, Grasshopper is ill-prepared and begs food from Ant. Ant refuses, so the Grasshopper starves to death. This abandonment of Grasshopper, in his time of great need, is the cause of Greene's complaints. Greene is repenting and is admitting he led a wasteful life, as the grasshopper did. In light of his repentance, he believes this does not justify being abandoned by his friends in his own hour of great need.

Greene, in Groatsworth, then instructs a further two people, presumably university men, who have *"writ against these buckram Gentlemen"*, not to *"maintain any more such peasants"*. Today, this line seems to be a contradiction; we need to read the word, *"against"* in its meaning of "alongside" to understand it. Buckram is the coarse fabric used to bind books. So, the so-called *"peasants"* are writers of published books who are probably actors too. This seems to be a dig at other "upstart" none university writers, similar to Edward Alleyn. In view of their literary partnership over the following years, I would put Michael Drayton, alongside Anthony Munday, as one pair of collaborators alluded to.

What Alleyn and/or Marlowe did in response, if anything, we don't know. To have-a-go at Chettle would be all they could do, Greene being dead and buried. Although Greene wrote most of Groatsworth, he may never have intended it to be published. He was getting it off his chest. This means that Henry Chettle was the true troublemaker.

Without that one phrase, "Shake-scene", Greene's Groatsworth of Witte would be long forgotten. It is not about London-Shakespeare.

Almost as soon as Groatsworth was printed there was (apparently) a dispute about whether or not Greene had anything to do with it. And if he did, how much of it was really his words and views? There also seemed to be a dispute about who Greene/Chettle was referring to. It seems that Henry Chettle had a success on his hands with Groatsworth, and learned that gossip and criticism sells publications. It appears that he decided to try his luck again by half revealing a theatrical secret.

Only a few weeks after the publication of Greene's Groats-Worth of Witte, Henry Chettle printed his own long, winding –and at times almost incomprehensible– story titled Kind Heart's Dream. Part of it refers to Munday and Shake-speare being joint authors.

The beginning, before the story, is an epistle headed in the standard form of the times, 'To the Gentlemen Readers'. It is a denial of wrongdoing in publishing Groats-worth of Witte. As regards the objections (allegedly) from the insulted authors, Chettle says he has met one and acknowledged he is a good man, but the other he has never met and never wishes to. I would assume that Marlowe is the one he has never met; but the one he has met, and put the record straight about, would be Alleyn. He already knew Nashe so it could not be him. Chettle denies he did anything wrong, saying it was all Greene's words and none of his. But then says he rewrote one of Greene's letters, and put something out but nothing in. Then adding,

18

"for the first whose learning I reverence, and at the perusing of Greenes Booke, stroke out what then in conscience I thought he in some displeasure writ".

He seems to be saying he removed an insult to the first person being insulted. That was, we believe, Marlowe. In this case, whatever it was, must have been far worse than saying he was an atheist because he kept that in Groatsworth. Perhaps, then, the insult was not against Marlowe and, so, not far worse than atheism. It could be connected to Alleyn, the removed insult may have been against theatre owner Philip Henslowe. Philip Henslowe was Edward Alleyn's father-in-law and is likely to have supported Alleyn's plays in his theatre. He, too, may also have been a friend of Greene's. Chettle would have had the common sense to drop Greene's (possible) insult of Henslowe, to avoid biting the theatrical hand that fed him.

Chettle then says the words in Groatsworth were, *"not mine nor Maister Nashe's"*. Considering that most people thought Nashe was young Junival in Groatsworth, this is rather mysterious. This whole supposed dispute may have been a publicity stunt encouraged by Chettle. All this sounds like an invented catch-all statement. Chettle is wriggling out of trouble by saying that if I have ever met you, but you haven't spoken to me about the insults, then it isn't you. Thus, all friends are still his friends. He then adds that Thomas Nashe was not the author of the epistle to the second part of the book, Gerileon. Chettle says it was himself who wrote the epistle and apologises to T.N. for the printer's error. This, supposed error, was only two letters, T.N. not a full name. Why he chooses to mention this non-incident at all is strange. It does not fit into the dispute about who wrote Greene's Groats-worth of Witte, nor into his Kind Heart's Dream story. The clue is in what he does not write. He does not say that the recently printed book, Gerileon, Part Two, was by Anthony Munday. He has contrived to mention *"Maister Nashe"* in order to then mention the T.N. mistake in Munday's, Gerileon. He is flagging up Munday's name in the minds of the readers, but without actually writing it.

Only four people are identified in the epistle that is intended to put the record straight. Henry Chettle himself, Robert Greene, Thomas Nashe and the writer of Part Two of Gerileon, Anthony

Munday. Nashe was Chettle's friend, and that is the reason to suggest he was involved with Chettle in writing Groatsworth of Witte. But what has Anthony Munday to do with it? Nashe is used as a vehicle to flag up Munday's name. Anthony Munday and Shake-speare are the men Chettle talks about in, Kind Hearts Dream.

After the epistle about Groatsworth, Chettle begins his new story. Of six characters that appear in Kind Heart's Dream, three names are real people; Richard Tarleton, Dr Burcot and Robert Greene, but these three were dead and gone. A fourth person, who is an unlucky and unfortunate fictional character from a Thomas Nashe story, is appropriately named Pierce Penniless (piss-poor). This leaves two, not readily identifiable, people named William Cuckoe and Anthony Now-now. Anthony Now-now we know is Anthony Munday because Chettle contrived to flag his name up in the introduction. Chettle chose these two names for a good reason. He wanted to imply "a Cuckoo in the nest." Thus, William Cuckoe is representing William Shakespeare, under the care and guidance of Munday. He is in Munday's nest and under his protective wing. Anthony Now-now is representing Anthony Munday. So, why did Chettle use Anthony Now-now for Anthony Munday?

In the very well-known 13th century song "Summer Has a Come on in", or sometimes called "The Cuckoo Song", the chorus is:

Sing **cuckoo now**, sing cuckoo,
Sing cuckoo, sing **cuckoo now**.

"Cuckoo" and "now" are sung together twice, Cuckoo-cuckoo and Now-now. The two names are sung as one. They are joined as one, so Chettle is saying they work together as one. This possibly points to Henry Chettle being side-lined as a co-writer by Munday. The inclusion in the story of Pierce Penniless' haunting presence would seem to represent Chettle's situation; as the grasshopper did for Robert Greene in Groats-worth of Witte.

In her book "Anthony Mundy–An Elizabethan Man of Letters", Celeste Turner also says (oddly, circumspectly) that Chettle is referring to Shakespeare and Munday in Kind Heart's Dream.

There can be little doubt that Kind Heart's Dream is combining the names William Shakspere and Anthony Munday. It would suggest that Chettle was penniless and possibly in debt and blaming others for his misfortune. These two publications, half revealing theatrical secrets, may have redeemed his finances.

Chettle's, Kind Hearts Dream, is, therefore, the first recorded allusion to London-Shakespeare that we know of.

A year later, in 1593, the poem Venus and Adonis was published. The name, William Shakespeare, was under the dedication. It was to Henry Wriothesley, the 3rd Earl of Southampton.

The name Wriothesley has a silent "W", as in Frank Lloyd Wright and Christopher Wren. It can be pronounced Roth-ez-lee or Riz-lee: but never, as Rio-the-sley.

This is the first use of the name, Shakespeare, on a work that there is a record of, and also the first London spelling of the name that is recorded. One year after that, in 1594, the poem, The Rape of Lucrecia was published. Again, it has William Shakespeare under the dedication to Henry Wriothesley.

"Our best plotter" is a unique complement to Anthony Munday in Francis Meres 1598 book, Palladis Tamia. Many subjects were covered in it, but what interests us is the section where he discusses literature. Under many differing headings, he critiques the works of writers ancient and modern and suggests the best. Shakespeare is mentioned nine times and some of the plays are listed:

Gentlemen of Verona, Errors, Love's Labour's Lost, Love's Labour's Won, Midsummer Night's Dream, Merchant of Venice, Richard the Second, Richard the Third, Henry the Fourth, King John, Titus Andronicus and Romeo and Juliet.

Francis Meres also strongly hints that he has met the author and he has been allowed to privately read some of the wonderful poems. This is eleven years before the sonnets were published. So, this man met London-Shakespeare and was allowed to read some of his unpublished work. This wasn't simply a handshake, it is social interaction with London-Shakespeare, but it is Anthony Munday he uniquely compliments?

21

In a section of his book under "So the best for comedy amongst us be," it begins a list of 17 authors, the first of which is: *"Edward, Earl of Oxford."* The list continues on and then ends with, *"...Greene, Shakespeare, Thomas Nash, Thomas Heywood, Anthony Mundye our best plotter, Chapman, Porter, Wilson, Hathway, and Henry Chettle."*

For some reason that has never been explained, Anthony Munday is given the unique high compliment, "our best plotter". Shakespeare does not receive any praise after any of his mentions. Some of the best plots are the Shakespeare plots; so, is Meres acknowledging that he knows Munday is bound up with the Shakespeare plays? That most of the credit for the plots lies with Munday? Is Munday our best plotter because of the Shakespeare play plots? And is he also our best plotter because he keeps his involvement with those plays a secret? No explanation other than this has been put forward. It is also odd that Meres uses Munday's full name, Anthony Mundye. The name, Shakespeare, does not have William put on the front of it, so why treat Munday as superior?

I am of the view that many of the plays were collaborations with other authors. The Two Noble Kinsmen, written by John Fletcher and William Shakespeare, was not unique. Thus, Munday-Shakespeare had help in writing them. I also believe that Francis Meres is telling us the names of those other authors. I partly base this belief on the two Munday plays whose authorship makeup is known. 'Sir John Oldcastle' and 'Sir Thomas More'. Five of the eight people mentioned by Francis Meres, after the name Shakespeare, in the above list, were involved in writing those two plays, and Munday was the lead author in both of them. Two plays are a tiny number to have scored so highly, referencing five authors from a, supposed, random listing of eight. It is a remarkable result. So, is Francis Meres telling us that all eight authors following the name Shakespeare in the list, were known to be contributory authors to the Shakespeare plays in 1598?

Were Nashe, Chapman and Porter also contributors to the Shakespeare plays and, therefore, sometime collaborators with the five known co-authors, Thomas Heywood, Wilson, Hathway, Henry Chettle and, of course, Anthony Munday our best plotter?

In Celeste Turner's 1928 book, Anthony Mundy. An Elizabethan Man Of Letters, the title of Chapter X1, is "OUR BEST PLOTTER". Astoundingly, the reference, "our best plotter", does not appear until four lines from the end of the last page of this chapter. Something happened before she published. Whatever it was, she deleted what she had originally written, but missed that she needed to change the chapter title. Referring to this compliment, the last line of chapter X1 is:

"It is no trifle to be exalted above such company!".

No trifle indeed, it is a massive, exclusive and intriguing compliment.

In her following chapter, but only one page on, she speculates what Ben Jonson must have felt about *"our best plotter"*.

"But it was disquieting to see such an old-fashioned botcher as Mundy set apart by three words of high praise: "Our best plotter".

We can pardon her for "old fashioned". She, like everyone else at that time, believed that Munday was eight years older than he actually was. But why does she need to immediately throw mud, *"botcher"*, at Munday's exalting compliment? Is it to confirm to whomsoever, her return to the accepted narrative in her previous chapter?

Francis Meres, following in Kind Hearts Dream's footsteps, contrived to reveal something extremely important to us. I believe that Celest Turner unravelled the truth in both of these publications. For some reason, she decided against revealing it and buried it. She was 21 years old and on the cusp of beginning her academic career.

Her hint, when explaining Kind Hearts Dream, that William Cuckoe (Shakespeare) and Anthony Now-now (Munday) were being portrayed together, motivated me to look deeper. It may be that the unchanged title, OUR BEST PLOTTER, was left as her deliberate marker, in the knowledge that her discovery will out one day. It now is out but 88 years later.

In the year 1599, Anthony Munday, with others, wrote a play titled Sir John Oldcastle. There is quite a story behind this. Three Shakespeare plays had a character named "Sir John Oldcastle". This man was a real person in history and he had a powerful family still living. His role in the plays was clownish and derogatory. He is–was in the three plays, Henry IV part I, Henry IV part II, and The Merry Wives of Windsor. It seems there were objections from his family to the way Oldcastle was portrayed, and also, from others because he was a Protestant Martyr. He was hanged and burned to death in 1417. I assume his descendants let the first two plays pass with a grumble, as they must have thought it was the end of it; both plays being about Henry IV. When Sir John Oldcastle then made another detrimental appearance in The Merry Wives of Windsor, they had had enough and must have objected with some venom. Something had to be done, so Munday wrote a play about the true life of Sir John Oldcastle, to put the record straight. The name of the character was then changed in the other three plays. It was changed to the now well-known, Sir John Falstaff. Shakespeare and Munday may have privately apologised to the Oldcastle family, we do not know, but if they did, it would be strange, because they inserted an unconvincing denial of it at the very end of the epilogue to King Henry IV part two.

"I know, Falstaff shall die of a sweat, unless already 'a be kill'd with your hard opinions; for Oldcastle died a martyr and this is not the man."

The first prints of Munday's Sir John Oldcastle play were not credited on the title page, but it was in the Printers' Register as Anonimus. A later print run of it was, however, credited to Shakespeare. We know that Munday, with others, wrote it because the payments for it are recorded as paid to them in Philip Henslowe's theatrical diary.

This 16 october 1599

Receved by me Thomas downton of phillipp
Henchlow to pay mr monday mr drayton & mr wilsson

& haythway for the first pte of the lyfe of
Sr Jhon Ouldcasstlle in earnest of the
Second pte for the vse of the company
Ten pownd J say receved.

So, why would Munday allow the play to be credited to Shakespeare? Whatever the reason, the two authors are shown to be working as one yet again. It is mystifying that among a great many playwrights mentioned in Henslowe's theatrical diary, Shakespeare is not there in any shape or form. Some of the early Shakespeare plays are mentioned as performed, but never that name. There is no good explanation of why not, other than the persistent claim that London's William Shakespeare, was actually someone's pen name. Munday came out of the debacle as Oldcastle's great defender, (our best plotter again).

Note: The single 'J' in the last line of Henslowe's diary (above), is an "I". The "J" sound was in the middle of evolving into a separate letter from "I", by having a curl at the bottom. Finding an "I" where a "J" should be is the norm. As an example, Ben Jonson's name was always printed as Ben Ionson. Thomas Downton seems to have adopted the change but has got it the wrong way around. "J" did not become standard English until 1633.

At Christmas 1598, the old "The Theatre" building in Shoreditch was dismantled, and the salvaged timbers moved into storage. The ownership of the actual building had been in dispute because the lease for the land it stood on had run out, and wasn't renewed. The dismantling was done in great secrecy while the landowner was away for Christmas, so it was a fait accompli when he returned to London. A few months later a new theatre was built mainly using these timbers; it was south of the river in Bankside. This new theatre was named, the now famous, Globe Theatre. It is said that Shakespeare was a sharer in this new theatre. Intriguingly, a globe is a representation of the world; "Repraesentationem Mundi" in Latin. The motto of the Globe is "Totus Mundus Agit Histrionem". In English, it is "the whole of the world plays the actor". Reading this

Latin as mock English, it is suggestive of "Tony Munday acts his stories". Is it the case that Shakespeare, Munday, and perhaps others, had a joint shareholding, but the holding was always referred to in Shakespeare's name? Was this one small way that shy Shakespeare could have his name in lights? Thus, having his name as a person pushed forward without mentioning Munday; but importantly, without having to meet anyone or appear in public.

In the year 1600, John Flasket published a book of poems named, England's Helicon. There are contributions from many poets, Lodge, Greene, Watson, Drayton, Oxford, Marlowe and others; known of, and not known. One poem is by W Shakespeare and there is also one by W.S. One poem is by Anonimus (there are others that are unattributed, and today we would say that they were anonymous too), one poem is by Sheepheard Tonie and six by Shep Tonie. These last eight are by Anthony Munday. Probably from his youthful travels incognito as Anthony Hawley in Europe, Munday was quite comfortable using aliases and pen names. He used several on his written works over the years. In 1578, a book was published titled "The Payne of Pleasure" by N. Britten. In this book is a dedication that is signed by A. Mundy. N. Britten was another of Munday's pen names to add to a list that includes Anonimus, Anglo-phile Eutheo, Lazarus Pyott, Anthony Gibson, Sheepheard Tonie, Shep Tonie and possibly, L. Digges. He also used his initials, A.M., as an author, and there may be other pen names as yet not identified.

The first poem in the book by Anthony Munday is, to me, the most enjoyable one. It may well be that it is simply still a pleasure to read today, whilst the style of the others has dated somewhat. On the other hand, it may be that it is the only alpha poem contributed to the book because it is the only one that is dedicated. Using the pen name Sheepheard Tonie, Munday contributed his poem Beauty Bathing. It is as follows:

To Colin Cloute.

Beautie sate bathing by a Spring.
Where fayrest shades did hide her.

The winds blew calme, the birds did sing,
the coole streames ranne beside her.
My wanton thoughts entic'dmine eye,
to see what was forbidden :
But better Memory said, fie,
so, vaine Desire was chidden.
Hey nonnie, nonnie. &c.

Into a slumber then I fell,
when fond imagination :
Seemed to see, but could not tell
her feature or her fashion.
But even as Babes in dreames doo smile,
and sometime fall a weeping :
So I awakt,as wise this while,
as when I fell a sleeping.
Hey nonnie, nonnie, &c.

FINIS.   Sheepheard Tonie.

The above is how it was originally printed, except that I have changed the old style long-S, which resembles this "*f*", to the modern "s".

Munday dedicated Beauty Bathing to Colin Cloute. He was a fictional character in Edmund Spencer's 1595 allegorical poem, "Colin Clouts Come Home Againe", about Spencer's time in London, and was probably meant to be Spencer himself. For Munday to dedicate a poem to Colin Cloute, would mean that he was actually dedicating it to Edmund Spencer. This would strongly suggest that Munday was one of the unidentified poets referred to in Spencer's poem. Munday had cleverly mirrored the compliment. The importance of this is that Edmund Spencer acknowledges Anthony Munday, to be one of the great poets writing in London at that time.

The Dawning

I do not know whether or not you, the reader, is ahead of me at this point. It is becoming clearer by the page, that the evidence is nudging us to see something different from Munday and Shakespeare being two authors working together. The evidence keeps on mounting up.

In the year 1600 Munday disappeared from the theatrical record for many months. It appears that he became seriously ill at that time.

There is a copy of Munday's "Palmerin of England, Part III" in the British Museum. The title page has the date 1602. There was a delay in bringing it to publication. It must have been a very long delay because Munday felt compelled to explain the reasons for it. In the paragraph after the dedication to a Maister John Swynnerton, Munday says:

"this long labour having cost me so many late and earlie hours among other mishaps of much bodilie sickness".

The illness must have been serious indeed if the residue afflictions dragged on and were still causing him problems over a year later. This was the time when London-Shakespeare's series of great tragedy plays began to be produced from his quill. The mystery of why London-Shakespeare began, in this period, to write about terrible tragic lives in his plays, has fascinated researchers for many years. It has never been explained. A serious illness of some kind has always been the most plausible explanation.

Some of the London-Shakespeare sonnets suggest that the author was lame. If Munday was lame, as the sonnets suggest, then it is possible that this may have been a consequence of the illness around 1600–1601. Munday's youngest child, Ann, died in childhood. We do not know when, but it is possible that they both caught the same serious illness and she did not survive it. This would be a double blow to Munday and could have pushed his move into deep misery much deeper.

28

The Book of Sir Thomas More is a handwritten and amended draft for a London-Shakespeare play. It refers to a manuscript book that is preserved in the British Library. It is the only known copy and no one knows how it came to survive when most other handwritten pages are lost. Its existence can only be traced back to 1728. [I discuss the preservation of this handwritten book in a later chapter]

The play titled Sir Thomas More is a play constructed from the working draft that is The Book of Sir Thomas More. It may have been fully written out as a performable play and performed after 1600, though it is considered unlikely. It was a lost play until the eighteenth century. If it had reached the stage of being finished then printed, it would have probably had Shake-speare on the title page. The first known professional performance of the play was in 1954.

It has been known since circa 1912, that The Book of Sir Thomas More was probably intended to be a play credited to London-Shakespeare. It is totally handwritten and no one disputes that the whole original draft of the play is in Anthony Munday's handwriting. It was an epiphany moment for all involved in Munday's handwriting's identification. For reasons known only to them; instead of shouting 'Eureka', they ignored the indication and searched the small, later, amendments to it. They then decided –for arcane reasons that I cannot work out– that one of those additions must belong to the elusive Stratford-Shakspere. It is not possible that those involved did not see that this play pointed strongly to the notion that Munday was London-Shakespeare, and this should have been discussed at length. It appears it was not discussed; and Munday was, for many years, relegated to 'probably' being a scribe for their, erroneous real author, Stratford-Shakspere.

We have to remember that no sentence in Stratford-Shakspere's handwriting exists anywhere. All there is are six signatures of his name from the end of his life, and all are different. There are many others that are now confirmed as forgeries. One of three signatures on his will says, "by me William Shakspere" but it is obvious that "by me William" is in a different hand to the word "Shakspere". He could not write. The scribe has written "by me William" and guided his hand to enable him to write "Shakspere".

There was, in the late nineteenth and early twentieth century, a tremendous blind-faith wave of desire to find something in Stratford-Shakspere's hand; anything, no matter how much reason had to be nudged aside.

The foul sheets that make up The Book of Sir Thomas More, with its additions, deletions, added sheets and with glued-in paper amendments, was re-discovered in the 1700s, but not fully analysed until 1912. There are, allegedly, seven different handwritings in the amended play. Five of them were designated as A.B.C.D.E. They later identified them to be A = Chettle, B = Heywood, C = the company bookkeeper, D = unknown and E = Dekker. There were also some comments censoring the manuscript in the hand of the Master of the Revels, then the handwriting of the whole original version by Anthony Munday.

It was –without a shred of supporting evidence– optimistically claimed by some that the supposed unknown writer could be Stratford-Shakspere. They suggest that Hand–D, as it is called, could be his, but that is grasping at straws. No sentence in his handwriting exists anywhere for comparison. Hand–D could be the hand of any one of a hundred other authors or scribes. Why would anyone consider it at all likely that it was Stratford-Shakspere's handwriting? The only handwriting of his that survives are six signatures, and they all look different, as though a scribe was guiding his hand; a common practice of the times. These signatures, if they are worth anything at all, rule him out as Hand–D, not in. There should be many other samples of his signature from his early and middle life, but none can be found. Could it be that he was not prosperous enough when younger to pay a scribe to guide his hand? Those many missing signatures may simply have been his mark, an X. If only one was recovered, it would, on its own, prove he was illiterate as many people believe.

The prevailing Stratfordian view about this play is based on no evidence. That view is that it was Munday's play, but Stratford-Shakspere was called in because the other four, professional and experienced authors, could not get it right. He –it is claimed– advised them and created and wrote the part that is Hand–D.

There is a strong body of opinion from studies of the handwriting, that Hand–C and Hand–D is actually the same person, the company bookkeeper; thus, Hand–D is, perhaps, not unknown. The reason to question this single hand theory is that Hand–C appears to have been written when much older. If it was the same man, then it is much more likely that the shift in handwriting was as a result of an injury to his hand or arm. Alternatively, it could be that Hand–D was written in autumn or spring and Hand–C in the freezing Elizabethan mid-winter while wearing fingerless mittens and by candlelight.

If it wasn't the bookkeeper's hand in both C and D, then there is a strong candidate that it is claimed could be Hand–D. Some of his handwriting is a close match to Hand–D and he was known to be involved with theatricals. Venus & Adonis and Lucrecia were dedicated to him by London-Shakespeare, and he is considered by some people to be the Fair Youth written about in the sonnets. He was Henry Wriothesley, third Earl of Southampton. It is unlikely that he composed the words of Hand–D; they will have been foul notes (much amended first drafts) from Munday, Chettle, Heywood or Dekker. His role would be as a copyist whose task was to produce a fair copy from the foul copy. It is known that Wriothesley was a patron of the arts and promoted, among others, the work of the above-mentioned author, Thomas Heywood. With this connection, Heywood could well be the author who created the foul copy, that Wriothesley's (possible) Hand–D is a fair copy of.

After Munday had finished writing the story, Sir Thomas More, it needed adapting, as all plays were, to create a play for the theatre. The main problem was that Munday's original play was too short. During this work, some parts were deleted and other parts created or extended, to allow for actors' wardrobe changes and scene changes. This is the stage that the Book of Sir Thomas More is at. That is to say, altered and shuffled about, to create a play that could actually be performed on a stage. There was nothing unusual about this development process; all London stage plays had to go through this amending for performance. It may never, at that time, have gone beyond the stage it is at today. To have taken it further, someone would have had to copy out many other sheets of paper; a plot sheet to be nailed up for everyone to follow during a performance. Then the individual sheets of dialogue for all the characters, and then the complete prompt book. None of these sheets exists, but if the play was ever performed, all of these sheets would have needed to have been copied out.

Strangely, there is nothing to suggest that Munday was involved in the later amending of his play after the Master of the Revels' objections. It could well be that the amending happened when Munday was seriously ill. This may be the reason why the three authors, Chettle, Heywood and Dekker were called in, and also why Harry Southampton, Wriothesley's preferred name among friends, was persuaded to help out as a copyist.

Munday is recorded as "our best plotter". Could it be that this play represents what often happened? Munday would write a short but complete play, then hand it on to others to be extended and modified, to create a play for theatre performance. Munday's second Robin Hood play, "The death of Robert Earl of Huntington", was a short play. It was later extended by Henry Chettle. This could partly explain how he appears in the record to be such a prolific author.

Munday's original, short play, of Sir Thomas More was generally considered to be mediocre because it did not flow and make good sense. Then, some years ago, an expert researcher who was studying the play sheets in the British Library, noticed that a worm had eaten into some of the pages but not all. With brilliant detective work, he deduced that one of the sheets was, unarguably, out of its original position. When it was moved into the correct position, the play then made sense. It was, as it always had been, a good little play.

It is a matter of contention that one of the three Hand–D pages was displayed in the British Library as the hand of William Shakespeare. The irony of that is that almost any other page has Munday's, therefore, Shakespeare's, handwriting on it; but not those three.

In 1603 Queen Elizabeth died. She was succeeded by James the First of England. James loved the Theatre and his endorsement of it no doubt helped everyone in the industry. He was enthusiastic about the performance of plays at court and asked for them to be performed regularly. He also changed the names of the main theatre groups. The Chamberlain's Men became the King's Men and The Admiral's Men became The Prince's Men. Until James The First, changed the mood, theatricals and the people involved in it were looked down upon.

Anthony Munday was a regular writer and producer of the City of London pageants. It is thought that he wrote and produced more than ten over the years. He wrote the whole performance then sold it to the authorities. He then hired the actors and singers, hired and provided the vehicles and sets, wrote and printed the souvenir booklets and arranged the passage of the parade through the streets. He then collected the money and paid the company and the bills. One of his pageants was to welcome the young Prince Henry to London. He was James The First's, eldest son and, therefore, heir to the throne of England and Scotland. He died of typhus at seventeen-years-old, so his younger brother, Charles, succeeded when James the First, eventually died. At the time, this pageant, for the then future King, must have been the commission of the year, and Munday was entrusted with it. He was a central figure in playwriting, poetry and performance art during those times. He was at the top of the tree. He was an impresario, not a lesser playwright, and being a hack was, as with most artists, a long-ago memory of youth and hunger.

In 1605 John Stow died. His literary executor was Anthony Munday. Stow had researched the history of London for many years. Many hours must have been spent in dusty guild archives, private libraries and muniment rooms. Then churches, streets, shops, and in conversations with older people who remembered the past. Stow published two editions of his Stow's Survay [sic] of London. The first was in 1598 and the second in 1603. Munday kept all of Stow's work in the next edition but added much to it. It was published as The Survay [sic] of London in 1618.

Stow had mentioned the new theatres in his 1598 book but dropped the reference in the 1603 edition because the two theatres mentioned in 1598 no longer existed. In Munday's first edition of

1618, he put the information back in, but it is the same, now completely out-of-date, original wording. Munday, it seems, could not bring himself to update theatres and entertainments. In 1633, the year of his death, his second edition of The Survey of London (survey as spelled today) was printed. He reprinted the same, out-of-date, theatre information:

"Of late time, in stead of those Stage-plays have been used Comodies, Tragedies, Enterludes, and Histories, both true and fained: for the acting whereof, certaine publike places have been erected."

Then, in a printed marginal note, of which there are several on most pages:

"Theater and Curten for Comodies and other shewes."

The Theatre building structure had been dismantled thirty-four years earlier. It had then been re-built as the Globe Theatre in Bankside. The Curtain Theatre went shortly after that. These two theatres had already gone before half of the then population of London were born, and Munday knew this. Why did he not change the theatre names to The Globe and The Fortune, that he knew were the main existing establishments? It would almost seem that he did not want the name, The Globe, recording in the book that logged everything else about London.

Was he shying away from revealing evidence that he knew anything about plays and playwriting? Why was he pretending that he didn't know that The Theatre and the Curtain Theatre had long gone?

Shakespeare's Sonnets 1609

In the year 1609, London-Shakespeare's Sonnets were published. These are remarkable in that they are as close to the man as we can get; they are a form of personal diary. I will not glaze over your eyes by going through my reading of them all. I can't anyway, because some seem to be simply emotional poems with no subject. Instead, I will point out some that I see as interesting. There does not seem to be a set overall order of production. Some of them may have been written thirty years earlier, and others three months earlier, than when they were published.

Anthony Munday, being London-Shakespeare, would almost certainly mean that some, if not all, of the "Fair Youth" sonnets, is about his son, Richard, and some of them make this plain. Richard Munday was taken to court over a paternity claim before he married. He was found not liable, though it does imply he was a normal active youth.

The dark lady in the sonnets is one of two women, his wife Elizabeth or Queen Elizabeth, although, I believe both of them are referred to in different sonnets.

To show how the wonderfully written sonnets are quite ordinary in their subject matter, I will summarise my reading of the first ten. They can almost be summed up as a group. Fall in love, marry, have children, be happy. It doesn't get any simpler.

Sonnet 1 – His wife Elizabeth is giving too much love to their children and thus depriving him of her love. The youngest child demands too much and she may be pregnant again.

Sonnet 2 – It is about his wife and their children as she grows older.

Sonnet 3 – About having children to renew yourself as your own mother did.

Sonnet 4 – His uxorious love for his wife, and the fear she will change.

Sonnet 5 – Beautiful summer flowers and trees blooming then dying in winter. A metaphor for life.

Sonnet 6 – Children are a joy, the more the merrier. Make children your heir, not the worms.

Sonnet 7 – The sun's passage across the sky as a metaphor for a man's life. You must have a son to repeat it.

Sonnet 8 – Man and wife should enjoy each other. A vibrating musical string will move the next string. Marry, have children and be happy.

Sonnet 9 – Marry and have children before you die. Your beauty of youth will be wasted otherwise. To not have love in your heart will destroy your ability to love.

Sonnet 10 – He has argued with his wife and asks her to cheer up and snap out of it.

I could be slightly wrong of course but not too far. Many of the other poems too, seem to say have children and particularly a son. Sonnet 13 ends "You had a father: let your son say so".

This, of course, does not mirror the life of Stratford-Shakspere in London. The (untrue) story is that he left or abandoned his family in Stratford-upon-Avon, to seek fame and fortune playwriting in London. There he stayed for over twenty-five years never moving his family to his new home. His plays became famous and he became prosperous. He then retired to Stratford-upon-Avon for his final years.

Those first ten sonnets cannot have been created by that fictitious London man from Stratford-upon-Avon. He would rarely, if ever, see his family. The love of family life in the sonnets makes no sense for a man who had dumped his family, and realistically, could not have had much to do with them. The real truth is that Stratford-Shakspere was indeed a loving family man, because he never left his family, never moved from Stratford-upon-Avon, and never went to write plays in London.

I believe that Anthony Munday met Queen Elizabeth many times. He served her all of his life from eighteen-years-old to her death in 1603. As he tells in The English Roman Life, he had an audience with Pope Gregory XIII. Not many Englishmen had ever met the Pope and Munday could describe him, his way of life, his court, the main men who served him and the rumours and talk in Rome. Queen Elizabeth was an intelligent woman and a polyglot herself. I see it as highly likely that she would want to hear the full details about her mortal enemy, from the man who had met him. The few foreign ambassadors who had met the Pope, would not be as forthcoming as a loyal subject. She would then have an advantage over them, in that she was reliably informed in truth and rumour. This may not have been Munday's first meeting with her, he had been a child actor when young and court performances were acted at royal command. If he did attend the Queen to tell what he knew, it would not be the last time. He was a poet, a singer, a songwriter, a musician, an actor, a playwright and a polyglot. He was a very interesting, entertaining, and trustworthy young man to have informally around her court occasionally. He was already in her employ as a Messenger of Her Majesties Chamber, and it is believed that two of his uncles also worked for the palace.

There are some sonnets that I believe are about Queen Elizabeth, two are reproduced below.

Sonnet 128
How oft, when thou, my music, music play'st
Upon that blessed wood whose motion sounds
With thy sweet fingers, when thou gently sway'st
The wiry concord that mine ear confounds
Do I envy those jacks that nimble leap
To kiss the tender inward of thy hand,
Whilst my poor lips, which should that harvest reap,
At the wood's boldness by thee blushing stand!
To be so tickled, they would change their state
And situation with those dancing chips
O'er whom thy fingers walk with gentle gait,
Making dead wood more blessed than living lips.
Since saucy jacks so happy are in this,
Give them thy fingers, me thy lips to kiss.

This is about a woman playing music that he has written. She is playing the virginal (a keyboard instrument) and he is proud and embarrassed at first, but then sees her adoringly as she sways and plays. Her fingers tickle the keys, and he wishes that they touched him.

A woman who had access to a virginal, could play it with skill, and also could read musical sheets, would be few and far between in Elizabethan times. It was Queen Elizabeth's favoured musical instrument.

Sonnet 130

My mistress' eyes are nothing like the sun;
Coral is far more red than her lips';
If snow be white, why then her breasts are dun;
If hairs be wires, black wires grow on her head.
I have seen roses damask'd, red and white,
But no such roses see I in her cheeks;
And in some perfumes is there more delight
Than the breath that from my mistress reeks.
I love to hear her speak, yet well I know
That music has a far more pleasing sound;
I grant I never saw a goddess go –
My mistress when she walks treads on the ground.
And yet, by heaven, I think my love as rare
As any she belied with false compare.

This is a brutal description of a woman that he adores. She is presumably quite old at this time. Munday was forty-two when the Queen died so younger when he wrote it. His wife would probably be circa thirty-seven when the Queen died and also younger when he wrote it. It does not ring true as a description of his wife in her thirties. Munday became an orphan at eleven-years-old so it was not about his mother.

We need to regard the words *"black wires"* as a distraction substitute; wire soon becomes rusted. He means auburn or red but dares not write that because it would strongly imply that he is referring to Queen Elizabeth. The sonnets were not published until after she had died.

In 1597, when she was sixty-five years old, Queen Elizabeth granted the French ambassador an audience. He recorded later that she opened her dress as though she was warm, and gave him a prolonged and ample display of her bosom. The ambassador wrote:

"and one can see the whole of her bosom..." then, *"her bosom is somewhat wrinkled as well as one can see for the collar she wears around her neck, but lower down her flesh is exceeding white and delicate, so far as one can see."*

He appears to be saying the skin below her bosom is exceedingly white, thereby inferring that her bosom isn't. If she did intend to expose her breasts deliberately, then they would have been made-up with powders to look their best and disguise the wrinkles, as her face would have been, before she had him summoned from the anti-chamber.

This may not have been a once-only reveal. Munday may have witnessed this himself at the time, or at some other time, or been told it by a courtier. He may, possibly, have read the ambassadors letter. He was once involved with spying and may well have been a trusted translator for Cecil's secret service. Any of the above would legitimise the line in the sonnet:

"If snow be white, why then her breasts are dun;"

Dun is a light brown-grey colour usually associated with horses and cattle.

There is a story about a rumour that Queen Elizabeth had died when young and the person on the throne as Queen, was actually a man in disguise. She was tall, intelligent and self-assured; she didn't marry and (apparently) had no children, so the rumour did make some sense. There is, therefore, the possibility that this mammary display was done to prove that rumour false. Considering she was sixty-five years old, it would seem to be rather late in the day to put the rumour to rest, but perhaps she wanted to remove all doubt, and ensure her historical legacy as the Virgin Queen. I find the changeling story itself impossible to believe, although it is true that there was a rumour to this effect. I can't come up with any other plausible reason for her to expose herself in a formal setting as she did.

39

Many of the Sonnets are about the weather in some form or other. That may be exactly what they are about, although it is much more likely that they are metaphors for life and becoming older. A great many of the sonnets seem to obsess about the passing of time and becoming old. Munday sometimes measures this ageing by seeing his own son growing up before his eyes. Sonnet 37 plainly begins this way.

As a decrepit father takes delight
To see his active child do deeds of youth

There is nothing ambiguous about these lines. The author is thinking about his son. Stratford-Shakspere's son died at eleven-years-old, so, he did not really become a youth. Munday died at seventy-two and his son, Richard, outlived him.

In Sonnets **37, 66** and **89** the author refers to lameness.

Sonnet 37:
As a decrepit father takes delight
To see his active child do deeds of youth
So I, made lame by Fortune's dearest spite, << **lame**
Take all my comfort of thy worth and truth;
For whether beauty, birth, or wealth, or wit,
Or any of these all, or all, or more,
Entitled in thy parts do crowned sit,
I make my love engrafted to this store.
So then I am not lame, poor, nor despis'd, << **lame**
Whilst that this shadow doth such substance give
That I in thy abundance am suffic'd,
And by a part of all thy glory live.
Look what is best, that best I wish in thee;
This wish I have; then ten times happy me!

The author seems to be saying that he is decrepit and lame now but takes delight in watching his son (Richard Munday) grow up into a man. Richard would be thirteen-years-old in 1600 when his father was seriously ill, he was on the cusp of becoming a youth.

The author is at peace with his lameness because he can see his son is like he was in youth. His son's vigour and accomplishments make him proud, and this in some way diminishes his own health issue, lameness. It does seem that he doted on his only son. As King Henry VIII plainly demonstrated, having a son was the most important thing to most men in those times, and for some people, into living memory today.

Sonnet 66:
Tir'ed with all these, for restful death I cry:
As, to behold desert a beggar born,
And needy nothing trimm'd in jollity,
And purest faith unhappily forsworn,
And gilded honour shamefully misplac'd,
And maiden virtue rudely strumpeted,
And right perfection wrongfully disgrac'd,
And strength by limping sway disabled,   << **limping. Disabled**
And art made tongue-tied by authority,
And folly, doctor-like, controlling skill,
And simple truth miscall'd simplicity,
And captive good attending captain ill—   << **he is ill.**
Tir's with all these, from these would I be gone,
Save that, to die, I leave my love alone.

The author seems to be going through a difficult time because he is ill. He sounds angry and depressed, suicidal almost. The last line would seem to refer to his wife, Elizabeth.

Sonnet 89:
Say that thou didst forsake me for some fault,
And I will comment upon that offence;
Speak of my lameness, and I straight will halt;   << **lameness**
Against thy reasons making no defence,
Thou canst not, love, disgrace me half so ill.
To set a form upon desired change,
As I'll myself disgrace, knowing thy will.

41

I will acquaintance strangle and look strange,
Be absent from thy walks, and in my tongue,
Thy sweet beloved name no more shall dwell,
Lest I, too much profane, should do it wrong,
And haply of our old acquaintance tell.
For thee, against myself I'll vow debate,
For I must ne'er love him whom thou dost hate.

The author talks of his lameness, but it appears to be more than that. Other physical problems seem to have been troubling him. It appears to suggest a speech impediment and/or general clumsiness from some illness. Whatever it was, he is struggling to correct and recover from it. The last two lines seem to refer to him disliking himself being this way, clumsy and disabled in gait and speech. That last line says he believes that his wife is a little unsympathetic to his afflictions.

This evidence of London-Shakespeare being lame in some way does not identify the man, but there are clues attached to the concept.

In his will, Stratford-Shakspere says:
"I William Shackspeare of Stratford upon Avon in the county of Warr gent in perfect health and memory god be praised do make and ordain …"
These words are specific, he says perfect health. This would not be true if he was lame and had other disabilities. There is nothing recorded in his life in Stratford-upon-Avon to suggest he was disabled, and no record of an illness about 1600, to account for the sudden lurch into writing tragedies.

Anthony Munday's will says:
"I Anthony Munday Citizen and Draper of London being very weak and feeble in body, but being sound and present in both mind and soul..."
This was a new will by Anthony Munday but it was not written in the few days or weeks before his death; he died four years after it was signed. He wasn't, therefore, dying when he signed his new will. The reason for writing a new will is made plain in it. Because he had

already been overgenerous to his children, he had decided to leave all of his diminished wealth to his second wife, Gillian. He wasn't bed-bound by this feebleness, however, because he worked on researching and editing his second edition of The Survey of London. "Weak and feeble", therefore, means what it says; mobility problems, rather than him being in poor health and near death. His 1633 publication of The Survey of London, was printed in the weeks after he eventually died on the 10 August 1633.

With Anthony Munday, we do know he was ill in the period 1600 – 1602 and this coincides with the lurch into the writing of the tragedy plays. The lameness may have been permanently inflicted on him by the illness. There is a supporting fact for Munday's lameness in his 1633 book, The Survey of London.

John Stow's "Stow's Survay of London" was published in 1593 and again in 1603. Stow died in 1605 and Anthony Munday became his literary executor. Munday published his own expanded edition in 1618 and named it "The Survay of London". He acknowledges in it that it is based on Stow's work. In all three of these books, the name of the ward in London, where he and other artists and writers lived, was spelled, Cripplegate Ward. Then, in 1633, Munday published a much enlarged and illustrated book, "The Survey of London", but in this edition, the name is changed to Creplegate Ward throughout. The Creplegate spelling was an old variant but it had fallen into disuse and become obsolete. Munday resurrected it.

Could Munday, by being lame, be offended by the word cripple. Did he decide to change it and try to remove it from London's history in his 1633 edition? Gate is a homophone of gait, meaning the manner in which someone walks, "Cripple-gait". Munday had lived in Cripplegate, was he name-called? Did he thoroughly hate it as most of us would? Publishing his book recording London in the fourth decade of the 17th century, gave him the opportunity to change things. Was he attempting to do that when, rejecting the "Cripplegate" spelling of the three previous editions, he changed it to "Creplegate"?

Anthony Munday did not use his full name on his two editions, he simply used his initials, A.M. in the title page; thus, his two editions did not become referred to as "Munday's Survey of London". He was trading on the popularity of the previous, ground-breaking publications, of Stow's Survey of London.

Sonnet 29 seems to be about his illness. It begins:
When in disgrace with Fortune and men's eyes,
I all alone beweep my outcast state,
And trouble deaf heaven with my bootless cries, etc.

It appears that he is infectiously ill and bedridden *"bootless cries"*, and possibly incontinent, ranting and without visitors, *"disgrace in men's eyes"* and *"all alone"* and it continues with him bemoaning he's not working while all about him are.

There are references in the sonnets to the name of the author, Shake-speare, being his pen name. Sonnets 72 and 81 do seem to say this. There are others, too, following this theme; 71, 72, 74 then 80 to 84 can all be read this way.

Sonnet 72:
O, least the world should task you to recite
What merit liv'd in me, that you should love
After my death, dear love, forget me quite,
For you in me can nothing worthy prove;
Unless you should devise some virtuous lie,
To do more for me than my own desert,
And hang more praise upon deceased I
Than niggard truth would willingly impart.
O, lest your true love may seem false in this,
That you for love speak well of me untrue,
My name be buried where my body is;
And live no more to shame nor me nor you!
For I am sham'd by that which I bring forth,
And so should you, to love things nothing worth.

The sonnet seems to be saying: I trust you as my closest love. If you love me, you will say good things about me and sanitise the truth when I'm dead. I don't want the shame on my name to live on (by

44

being attached to Shake-speare). Everyone will forget me and my shame and it will not taint you or my Shake-speare.

Again, in Sonnet 81, the real author is talking about his famous pen name.

Or I shall live your epitaph to make, (If I am given the chance before I die I will kill off my Shake-speare.) This is exactly what the real author did when he published the First Folio of thirty-six plays in 1623.

Or you survive when I in earth am rotten; (Or I die before I have a chance to kill it off.)

From hence your memory death cannot take, (Shake-speare is far too famous now to be forgotten.)

Although in me each part will be forgotten, (No one must know that I wrote as Shake-speare or the name will be tainted by my name.)

Your name from hence immortal life shall have, (Shake-speare will never be forgotten.)

Though I, once gone, to all the world must die, (I must ensure that my name dies with me and not be linked to Shake-speare.)

The earth can yield me but a common grave, (I don't want to be celebrated as the author "Shake-speare" in death.)

When you entombed in men's eyes shall lie. (Though your name will live on in the minds of mankind.)

Your monument shall be my gentle verse, (The words I wrote under your name will be your monument.)

Which eyes not yet created shall o'er-read; (And those words will be read by future generations.)

And tongues to be your being shall rehearse, (And the plays performed by future generations.)

When all the breathers of this world are dead. (When everyone alive today has died.)

You still shall live, such virtue hath my pen, (My words will endure and give my Shake-speare immortality.)

Where breath most breathes, even in the mouths of men. (My Shake-speare will be loved in the hearts of all. Everyone will quote it.)

He is saying that the author named in this book of sonnets, Shake-speare, is not his real name. He, the real author, wants his name to die with him. He is tainted by something and does not want that taint to be attached to his writings as Shake-speare; as it would be if it were known that he was the real author. That big taint is unknown but it must have been something serious. The only things serious enough at that time are that he was in a relationship with another man. Or he was close to another person who both declared and discussed atheism. Either of these wrongs must have still been a secret when he wrote the words, otherwise, action would have been taken against him. So, why would he think that it would be revealed and proved at his death, and possibly taint his pen name, Shake-speare?

There is one other thing that could be the cause of his taint and crucially, unlike the other two, it was already known about. In the case of Anthony Munday, it could be his well-documented work as a government agent and pursuivant of Catholics and Puritans, working under the psychopath, Richard Topcliffe. This led to many priests and people being taken, fined or imprisoned; and to some of those being tortured and hanged. His peripheral part in the punishment of many people lasted years, and he wrote about it. He was disliked, if not hated for it by some. I believe he did it out of loyalty to his Queen and Country, but he may have been coerced to do it. He did, after all, almost become a Catholic priest in Italy; or, he may simply

46

have done it for the money. Whatever the truth, it appears he was criticised for it and, in later life, after Queen Elizabeth died, was regretful. Topcliffe died in 1604, that one man's death may have partly liberated Munday from this past.

There is another very simple thing that could be the cause of his disowning his writing for the theatre. Puritanism was on the rise. Did he simply become very religious? Could he be misinterpreting his disabilities as punishment from God? Was it because he was now ashamed of his bawdy writings, his connections with public entertainments and his pageants? His gravestone inscription, surprisingly, mentions none of these things.

In 1616 the great Philip Henslowe died. He is the man to thank for leaving us his theatrical diary that is a treasure chest of information about Elizabethan and Jacobean theatre. It is preserved in Dulwich College.

A man named William Shakspere, who lived in Stratford-upon-Avon, also died in that year. No one in London noticed. No one wrote anything at all about his death. If he had been London-Shakespeare he would have been celebrated and buried in Poets' Corner in Westminster Abbey, as many other lesser poets were.

Droeshout Portrait 1623

In 1623 a remarkable book was published that contained 36 plays authored by London's William Shake-speare. It has been referred to as the First Folio of Shake-speare Plays ever since. Folio refers to the physical size of it; approximately 12.5 inches by 8.5 inches (318 mm x 216 mm). It is thought that 750 copies of the First Edition were printed. Essentially, it appeared from nowhere. Many of the plays are not recorded before they appeared in this book, though they must have been performed previously. In the introduction, homages are paid to the author Shake-speare and he is referred to as already being dead, but it does not mention when he died or where his grave is. Everything is vague. Ben Jonson seems to be the main mourner and celebrant involved. The actors and theatre managers, Heminge and Condell, have their names appended to eulogies, although it is considered doubtful that they actually composed them. In our search for the real London-Shakespeare, we are interested in several pieces of evidence contained in, what is, the fundamental treasure chest of all Shakespearian knowledge, The First Folio of Shake-speare Plays.

In Ben Jonson's long elegy to Mr William Shake-speare, he says he had met the author's children. He makes mention of London-Shakespeare's issue in this elegy. It makes it plain that he had met them and that he knew them. He is also saying that many other people knew London-Shakespeare's children too. Lines 64 to 67 are:

"For a good Poet's made, as well as borne.
And such wert thou. Looke how the fathers face
Lives in his issue, even so, the race
Of Shakespeares minde, and manners brightly shines"

Jonson was the master of ambiguity, so, the words can mean different things.

If the four lines are, in spite of the full-stop/period, all one statement, then Jonson is saying that London-Shakespeare's father was a known poet and that he looks like him. This excludes Stratford-Shakspere.

If, as I believe, it is two statements that split at the full stop/period, then the first sentence says he is a self-made poet. The second says that Jonson, and others in London, knew London-Shakespeare's children (middle-aged children by this time). So, London-Shakespeare lived in London with his family. In addition, it would not make sense to say this, *"looke..."* seven years after Stratford-Shakspere had died, and ten years after he had, allegedly, left London. Again, this excludes Stratford-Shakspere. It does make sense when said about Munday.

In line 66 are the words *"even so"*. They seem strange unless you read them as meaning that the father is not dead.

Jonson's other dedicatory poem in the First Folio, To the Reader, is in the prime position facing the Droeshout portrait. It contains 272 letters.

To the Reader.

This figure, that thou here seest put
It was for gentle Shakespeare cut;
Wherein the Graver had a Strife
With Nature, to out-doo the life:
O, could he but have drawne his wit
As well in brasse, as he hath hit
His face; the Print would then surpasse
All, that was ever writ in brasse.
But, since he cannot, Reader, looke
Not on his Picture, but his Booke.

In a discussion thread attached to the short online course, "Who Wrote Shakespeare?" Tutored by Dr Ros Barber, an anomaly was pointed out by one of my fellow students. In 2007, Mr C. Gamble wrote that he had discovered, against the odds, the letter 'm' was missing from the poem. Other students, motivated by this, soon pointed out that five other letters, j,q,x,y and z, were also missing. Four of these letters, j,q,x and z, occur, on average, on much higher letter counts in written English. 'j', the most common of these four letters, only occurs, on average, every 653 letters. Thus, their absence from the 272 letters-long poem is not significant. The letter 'y' is different.

Letter 'y' occurs, on average, every 50 letters. So, over five times in 272 letters; but it does not appear in the poem at all.

Letter 'm' occurs, on average, every 41 letters. So, over six times in 272 letters; but it, as Mr Gamble discovered, does not appear in the poem at all.

It seems that Ben Jonson has highlighted the letters 'm' and 'y' by omission from his poem. My view is that this omission is deliberate. The letters 'm' and 'y' begin and end the name, Munday. They are pointing us to two of the clues in the Droeshout picture puzzle on the facing page to the poem.

The ubiquitous portrait of London-Shakespeare printed in the First Folio is called the Droeshout portrait because it was cut into the brass printing plate by the sculptor, Martin Droeshout. His name is at the bottom of every print of it in a First Folio. Droeshout, however, did not draw the picture; it was not good enough to be by him because it simply isn't correct. The reason it isn't correct is not that the real artist could not draw properly. It is because the portrait is a picture puzzle that includes pointers to who the real London-Shakespeare is. The most likely candidate as the artist is Anthony Munday's son, Richard Munday, who was a freeman of the Painter–Stainer Guild, and is mentioned in heraldic records as a researcher. This theory, that there are clues pointing to the real author hidden in the picture, is not new. It has long been claimed that there are things wrong with the portrait. Most people accept that the two arms shown, are in fact, the front and the back of the same arm. Thus, only one arm of the man is shown, suggesting that another person is hidden in the picture. The crescent moons under the eyes and the shiny patch on the forehead have been long discussed as strange. The odd-looking, unrealistic collar around the neck, has also been studied in great detail as some kind of message or clue. The spikes and spacings on the collar have been measured and tabulated to reveal the clues. One torturous mangling of the data has even produced Queen Elizabeth as the author of Shake-speare. Considering that paper can expand and contract with damp or dry conditions, and can even vary as the brass plate is repeatedly printed, means this microanalysis is pointless. The clues are designed to be consistent whatever the conditions, and from first print to last print.

In addition to the obvious "one arm" indication of something being concealed in the portrait, there are other pointers.

The first is the crescent moons under the eyes, the shiny patch on the forehead and the shadow to the side of the head. The crescent moons simply imply "moon". The bright shiny patch on the forehead –in a time when there were only oil lamps, candles or daylight– has to be reflected daylight. It says it is daytime. The only purpose to its un-aesthetic appearance on the forehead is to imply "day". The shadow to the side of the head is also implying "day". So, moon and day, moonday; Monday. The same clue repeated twice.

Revealingly, the shadow was not on the first prints to come off the printing press. The Folger collection holds 82 First Folios, only two of them have no shadow to the side of the head. The print run was stopped after pressing fewer than two dozen copies. The brass plate was removed from the printing press and taken to Droeshout's workshop to be altered. They did not request the obvious; to tone-down the shiny patch on the forehead. Instead, they asked Droeshout to cut a shadow to the side of the head. It can only have been done to balance the clues and re-enforce the word 'day' a second time. Moon-day, Monday, a homophone and alternate spelling of Munday.

The second pointers are in the embroidered borders of his jerkin. There is a large "m" across the whole chest. As highlighted by omission from Jonson's poem on the facing page to the portrait.

The right side of the "m" also forms an "n".

The strange, unrealistic, mysterious and much-discussed collar around the neck is simply a large letter "D".

From the neck down, the borders are seen to form a "Y". Again, as highlighted by omission from Jonson's poem on the facing page.

"m n D Y". Add the vowel and it's Mundy. It is as prosaic as that and has been hiding in plain view for almost 400 years. These pointers will not change with humidity or distorted printing.

Admittedly, I have the advantage of the same name, and that has helped me to identify these clues. Even so, I have serious doubts that I am the first person in 390 years to de-code this picture puzzle. I am convinced that John Paine Collier, for one, knew about it. I believe he came across evidence that Munday was Shake-speare. With that knowledge, he would very soon interpret the clues in Droeshout. He could not bring himself to believe it, but could not explain it away. He concealed it, then spoke of Munday in derogatory terms, and that has continued to this day. There must have been other discoverers too. The theatrical history of the times is shot-through with the name, Anthony Munday. When searching for the missing author, London-Shakespeare, some enthusiasts must have researched Munday as the possible author.

Many people, who deny that there is a London-Shakespeare authorship problem, do not like to discuss the Droeshout portrait (and the later, Marshall portrait). This is because the Droeshout portrait is solid-gold evidence from the First Folio of London-Shakespeare's plays. As such, it outranks contradictory sources of evidence because it cannot be wrong. The decoding of the picture puzzle is there to see and it shouts one name. It has to be explained away by people who don't agree with it. The problem is the deliberate and undeniable back-to-front arms. It is plainly there to see and must have a purpose. That purpose is to tell us that there are two people in the picture, one of whom is concealed. The outcome of staring at the picture, knowing that the letters m and y are significant, is to confirm that it is the solution to the puzzle, it reveals the simple truth. Anthony Munday was London-Shakespeare.

Mr. WILLIAM
SHAKESPEARES

COMEDIES,
HISTORIES, &
TRAGEDIES,

Publifhed according to the True Originall Copies.

*The following images are by permission of the Folger Shakespeare
Library under a creative commons share-alike protocol.*

The 1623 Droeshout Portrait of Shakespeare/Munday
From the First Folio of thirty-six Shakespeare Plays.

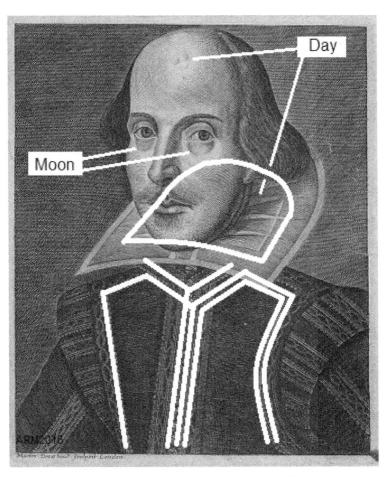

The 1623 Droeshout portrait of Shakespeare/Munday
A rebus for Moon twice and a rebus for Day twice

The letters m n D Y are highlighted

This interpretation of the Droeshout portrait is simple and straightforward. It is the smoking gun on its own, but to leave us in no doubt, it is fully supported and overwhelmingly validated by the Marshall portrait at a later date.

On the 10th of August 1633 Anthony Munday, and therefore, Our Shakespeare, shuffled off his mortal coil at almost seventy-three years old. This was the same year that his, The Survey of London, was published for the second time. His assistant and co-editor, Humphrey Dyson, managed to insert Munday's epitaph inscription into it. The epitaph in the book is the only record of it, as the church of St Stephen in Coleman Street, where Munday was interred, was burned to ruin in the Great Fire of London in 1666. Anthony Munday's ashes and, therefore, William Shakespeare's ashes, lie in the ground under 36 Coleman Street in the City of London. There is a commemorative plaque marking the site of Saint Stephen's Church on the building opposite King's Arms Yard.

Munday's tomb inscription is as follows:

To the memory of that ancient servant to the city,
with his pen, in diverse imployments,
especially the Survay of London,
Master Anthony Munday,
citizen and draper
of London.

He that hath many an ancient tombstone read
(Ith labour seeming more among the dead
To live, than with the living)
that survaid obstruse antiquities , and oer them laid
Such vive and beauteous colours with his pen,
That (spite of time) those old are new agen,
Under this marble lies inter'd: His tombe,
Clayming (as worthily it may) this roome,
Among those many monuments his quill
Has so reviv'd, helping now to fill A place (with those)

56

in his survay: in which He has a monument, more faire, more rich,
Than polisht stones could make him, where he lies,
Though dead, still living, and in That nere dyes.

Obiit Anno Ætatis suæ 80. Domini 1633. Augusti 10.

Anthony Munday will have written his own epitaph in order to keep
his secret and not be unmasked as London-Shakespeare. If left to
others they may have felt compelled to reveal the secret. It may be
that had he known how long he was going to live, he may not have
been so concerned about hiding his London-Shakespeare writings.
He was 62 years old when the First Folio was published and he
would have believed his time was very near. Within a few years,
many of the people he thought may attach his decried spying and
government activities to his Shakespearian writings had predeceased
him or were old and inactive. His self-authored tomb inscription
must have been given to someone for safekeeping, presumably his
second wife, Gillian, or his son. He cannot, of course, have written
the last line. There is an error in that last line. He was almost 73, not
80. This caused historical dating problems for many years until his
baptism record was found. It confirmed that he was baptised on 13
October 1560. The only allusion to his books, poems, plays and
pageants is in the second line. It seems he was content to be
remembered only for The Survey of London. He eschewed all
reference to his other written works to the very end; all of the many
works under his own name as well as the Shake-speare canon.

The last contemporary first-printing of a Shake-speare play was
The Two Noble Kinsmen in 1634, a few months after Munday's
death. There is an intriguing story about this play and Munday's two
extant handwritten plays, "John a Kent and John a Cumber" and "Sir
Thomas More". These two handwritten plays, by Munday, were
rediscovered separately, but both are covered in the same velum
salvaged from an older book. Both books have matching staining and
damage. They had been stored together, in poor conditions, for years.
Logic says that they were stored and ignored at the bottom of a chest
in Munday's workroom. After he died in 1633 his widow, Gillian,

will have sold them on to a bookseller, who must have sold them on to separate customers. This is how these two rare, handwritten, Elizabethan plays have survived against all the odds.

The last London-Shakespeare play to be contemporaneously first printed was The Two Noble Kinsmen in 1634. It appeared from nowhere a few months after Munday died. Was this play in the chest as well? Sadly, it is probable that the handwritten sheets would have been recycled soon after printing. If it had been sold to a bookseller instead of a printer, those handwritten sheets would still be extant, and the world would have always known that Anthony Munday was London-Shakespeare.

This does, however, raise a tantalising question; if Gillian Munday sold two handwritten plays to a bookseller for the profit, then it would be reasonable to believe that the printer of The Two Noble Kinsmen, or one of his men, would have done the same after printing; it would be a nice little earner on the side. Can it be that the handwritten sheets of The Two Noble Kinsmen are still extant in a dusty archive somewhere, possibly hidden by being bound in with other works?

To be frivolous for one paragraph; In the cartoon series, "The Simpsons", the writers have correctly predicted the future many times. The weight of the Higgs-Boson, Greece's debt default, a Nobel Prize winner, Donald Trump becoming President, and many other things. They have also predicted that The Two Noble Kinsmen is extant. Sadly, they showed Moe, who claimed he had a Shakespeare play, wiping his tears away with The Two Noble Kinsmen when he realised, he had sold a bottle of wine too cheaply. The dichotomy of values being the joke, presumably. Let us all hope that Matt Groening and his team have got it correct once again.

Marshall Portrait 1640

In 1640 the book of poems titled "Poems: Written by Wil. Shake. Speare. Gent." was re-published. The literary style had moved on, the original, 1609 form of presentation of them was considered old fashioned. Thus, the sonnets were mixed up and combined, so they do not reproduce an exact facsimile of the sonnets as originally published. A new portrait of the author was drawn and printed within this book.

It is probable that Munday's surviving children, Elizabeth, Priscilla and Richard, were the people behind this book being published again. Richard would, almost certainly, be the artist who drew the design for William Marshall, the sculptor, to cut onto a brass plate for printing. This 1640 portrait of London-Shakespeare, contains further proof of the true identity of the pen-name Wil Shake.Speare. It is significant and deliberate that the name reverts to being spelled in hyphenated form, as it was in the early days. It suggests it is a pen name.

Richard's first thought when creating the design seems to have been to imitate the Globe Theatre and include a representation of the world, "Repraesentationem Mundi" in Latin. He drew an oval with clouds surrounding it. The oval is a wide band that has a white daytime side on the left and a black nighttime side on the right. A hatched segment at the bottom represents the earth we walk on, and a large crescent moon is in the sky

Once again only one arm of the man is drawn, so suggesting there is another person in the picture.

Across the chest once again are letters from the family name, an "M" formed by the cloak's edge. An "N" formed half by the cloak and half by the left edge of the buttons' placket down the chest; note how the knuckles of the hand carry the left side of the placket down to form the "N". The "A" is formed by the right side of the button's placket and the arm on the right. Around the neck is the same strange collar as Droeshout's engraving, forming the "D" again. The "D" collar has a joint drawn off centre that points down the line of buttons. It indicates that the "D" fits between the "N" and the "A". MNDA. MuNDA. Munday.

The crescent moons under the eyes, the reflected daylight on the forehead, and the shadow to the side of the head are used as in the Droeshout image and are, once again, saying "Moon" and "Day", Monday, a homophone and alternate spelling of Munday.
To reinforce these symbols and leave us in no doubt, it is repeated again. The large, unignorable, crescent moon to the left of the head and shoulder is sitting to the left of the shiny patch on his forehead. In this portrait, it shouts "Moon" - "Day". Monday.

Having added another reference to 'moon', Richard adds another reference to "day", to complete three pairs of symbols this time. The lower half of the laurel leaves below the hand is shown casting a shadow on the earth.

On the shiny chest of the tunic, one each side of the buttons, are two large disguised letters, a "C" and a "P". They stand for Catholic and Protestant; a direct reference to Anthony Munday's lifetime work for Queen and Country. These two letters are iconic of Munday's life. The "C", indicating Catholic, is demonised by being bat-like, thus seeming to suggest "Of the Night".

A hand that is too small holds one laurel leaf stem. Not enough to rest on, at least half is missing, the Munday half.

Finally, there is part of Ben Jonson's elegy to Shake-speare copied from the 1623 First Folio. It has been amended. Where the original had exclamation marks, this one has question marks, throwing doubt on this picture being Shake-speare and on the praises to Shake-speare.

This Shadow is renowned Shakespear's? Soule of th'age
The applause? delight? the wonder of the stage.

Richard Munday and his sisters commissioned William Marshall to sculpt the image onto a brass plate for printing in the book. Their father's poems were published again in 1640, with the William Marshall engraving.

POEMS:
WRITTEN
BY
WIL. SHAKE. SPEARE.
Gent.

This Shadowe is renowned Shakespear's Soule of th'age
The applause! delight! the wonder of the Stage.

1640 Marshall portrait of Shakespeare/Munday

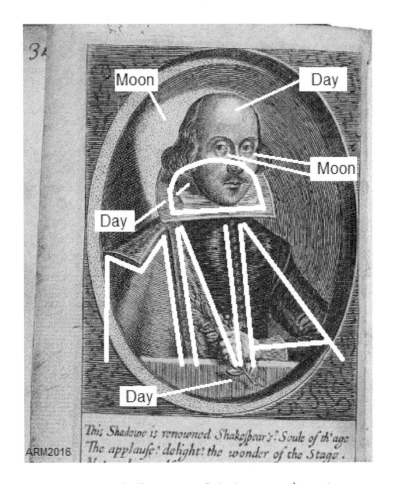

This Shadowe is renowned Shakespear: Soule of th'age
The applause: delight: the wonder of the Stage.

1640 Marshall portrait of Shakespeare/Munday

A rebus for Moon thrice and a rebus for Day thrice
The letters M N D A are highlighted
C for Catholic and P for Prostestant are on the chest

63

This solving of the 1640 Marshall portrait puzzle is the second smoking gun. It shouts the identity of the true author of London-Shakespeare and fully validates the solving of the Droeshout portrait puzzle.

Richard Munday's Droeshout Portrait came first in 1623 and it uses four letters: M. N. D. Y. to represent the name Munday. It also uses the moon and day symbols to represent Monday. Richard Munday's Marshall Portrait uses the letters M. N. D. A., so he changed the last letter. Although changed, it is still a perfect phonic indicator of the name Munday; it is both an alteration and a confirmation. It then re-enforces the moon & day symbols by repeating them a third time to leave us in no doubt. There is a large, unmistakable, unignorable, crescent moon to the left of the head. This is Richard Munday, now a little freer of his father's cloak of secrecy, ensuring that his father is identified as London's William Shakespeare.

Richard would be well aware that King Charles the First was at loggerheads with Parliament because he had kept it closed down for many years. He was, thus, usurping Magna Carta. What no one knew was that the English Civil War was only two years away, and everything would be changed. The Parliamentarians, fighting for a return to Magna Carta democracy, won the war, and Charles the First was subsequently beheaded. Cromwell and his Puritans ruled until his death in 1658. The monarchy was, eventually, restored and Charles the Second was crowned King in 1660, one hundred years after the birth of Anthony Munday. During those eighteen Puritanical Cromwellian years, theatres and the English Renaissance were crushed. Those few remaining people, who knew that Anthony Munday was London-Shakespeare, were in possession of a worthless theatrical secret that soon died with them.

Remnants and Remains

I find it difficult to believe that J.P. Collier did not uncover the truth in the 1800s. If he did, he decided to wipe it out and did three things.

The first was to place forgeries into the historical record, in order to show that Stratford-Shakspere had been in London.

The second action was to follow in the footsteps of Kind Heart's Dream and Parnassus, denigrating Munday to make it appear that he was not good enough to have written Shake-Speare.

The third action was to destroy letters and papers that strongly suggested, or even proved, that Stratford-Shakspere was not London-Shakespeare. There must have been dozens of private letters written mentioning that Shake-speare was a pen name, or even who the real London-Shakespeare was. It is human nature to blab a small secret – and at the time, that's all it was– in the expectation it will impress friends. Chettle and Nashe, as we know, revealed the secret in Kind Hearts Dream. Collier may even have discovered handwritten London-Shakespeare play sheets in the libraries he had access to. He would know full well whose handwriting it was because he'd had Munday's handwritten, John a Kent and John a Cumber, in front of him.

The first two of these accusations are true; the third one is not provable.

Late in his life, long after he had been exposed as a forger, Collier said;

"I have done many base things in my time-some that I knew to be base at the moment, and many that I deeply regretted afterwards and up to this very day."

There must be undiscovered forgeries that he is referring to, but not a great number. He, though, uses the word "many" twice. In the quote above he says, *"and many that I deeply regretted afterwards and up to this very day."* If he *"deeply regretted"* it, he could have quietly put it right at any time before he was exposed. At that time, he was one of the main men. This statement, drawn out of him towards the end of his life, therefore, suggests an action that can't be undone, like throwing on a fire. Forgery of or on a document can be undone with a full confession. I believe that the reason he never made a confession, was because he knew if he did, he would be continually cross-questioned about it and the truth will out. So long as he refused to say anything, no one could assemble the truth and discover that he had, unforgivably, destroyed historical evidence. He took the knowledge of his forgeries and the destruction of historical evidence to the grave.

Anthony Munday toured through France to Italy in 1578 and returned in 1579. His book about this journey, The English Romayne Lyfe, was published in 1582. It tells of his adventures and the people he met. As he did with his later London-Shakespeare writings, he introduces new words.

BRASEN: The etymology of the word brazen is recorded as originating from the 1570s. Munday's use of the word brasen (brazen) seems to mean a rock made of brass, more probably a rock encased in brass sheet, that is claimed to be something it isn't.

"In the entrance to St Peter's Church there is a stone made of brass that the Friars claim to be the rock that our saviour stood on when he told Peter that, "Upon this rock I shall build my church". The saviour meant himself when he spoke those words, and not by Peter. This piece of brass they make the ignorant to believe to be that rock. The people drop to their knees and pray to this brasen rock."

It would seem that Munday created the word brazen in the sense of meaning, without shame.

CARNIVAL: In Philip J. Ayres' edition of The English Roman Life, he points out that Munday describes the three-day celebrations as Carne Vale, meaning put away meat for Lent. So, it seems he also introduced the word Carnival into English.

The London-Shakespeare plays are quoted endlessly. Many of the Shakespearian quotes would be copied from older works, some would be new creations and others in common use but not previously written down. The following are a small sample from Munday's 1580 book, Zelauto: The Fountain of Fame, written when he was only nineteen-years-old.

That man is very wise that never offended in folly.
That man is very valiant who never meets with his match.
A bad excuse (they say) is better than none at all.
Where no better is, bad will suffice.
If it be to be gotten in Naples for love or money, you shall have it.
A friend in necessity: is better than a hundred in prosperity.
Faint heart never won fair lady.
All is well that is well taken.
Little said is soon amended.
For you were better beware before: then wish you had taken heed, when it is too late.
Saying and doing are two men's labours.
He's as churlish as an old horse gnabling on a thistle.(contracted)
That comes in an hour: that happens not in seven years.
The sun should not set on an anger conceived.
He began to smile in his sleeve.

There are many more and are all listed in Jack Stillinger's edition of Zelauto, The Fountain of Fame.

The word Anonimus was created by Anthony Munday as a pen name. It is a compound word that did not, originally, mean unknown. It is made up of the two words; anon and Imus.

Anon is an archaic English word that means "soon". It is still sometimes heard today in the phrase, "I'll see you anon."

Imus is a Latin word that means "we go".

Anon-imus, therefore, has a meaning of "soon we go", more usually expressed as "life is short"; a common theme in the London-Shakespeare Sonnets. It carries a similar meaning to the well-known Latin phrase that hints at his name, *"sic transit gloria mundi"*. It translates to, "thus passes the glory of the world", or, more informatively nowadays, "worldly things are fleeting", thus, "soon we go".

Munday's reasoning behind the creation of this pen name seems to be that he wanted to build it out of his own name. If we write "Anthony Munday's play" (or poem, or book) we find the pen name, Anonimus, laced through it.

Anthonie Munday's play
An oni mu   s

The letters 'y' and 'ie' were more loosely interchangeable in those times, and there are records of Munday spelling his name Anthonie. One such is his famous 1582 book, The English Romayne Lyfe, which is the story of his time living in France and Italy when eighteen years old. It was probably written when nineteen years old. He signs at the beginning and at the end of the book as Anthonie Munday.

The word Anonimus was re-interpreted as meaning unknown sometime after Munday, retrospectively, changed the authorship of the early plays from Anonimus to Shake-speare. Theatrical enthusiasts, knowing that the early plays were originally by Anonimus, but had subsequently reappeared as by Will Shake-Speare, wrongly assumed that Anonimus must have meant unknown or concealed. The pen name change may have marked the point at which Munday moved on from writing alone, to writing the plays as collaborations with other authors. An anonymous work was, in Elizabethan times, either left unattributed or signed as Ignoto; the Latin word for unknown. The spelling and changed meaning eventually evolved to today's word, anonymous. I believe that Munday created this pen name when very young. There is a schoolboy –faffing about with his name and his Latin– feel to its creation.

There is an extant record of Munday using the pen name Anonimus. In the late 1590s, Munday translated a book titled A Woman's Worth. The book is credited to Anthony Gibson but it was a pen name of Anthony Munday. He then comments in the book about what is his own work but signs the comments as by Anonimus. He has translated a book, published it under a pen name, and then commended it in a comment under a second pen name.

The word also appears in John Flasket's, England's Helicon. This book of poems is remarkable for the reasons discussed previously, but also because, oddly, it has both forms of the words meaning "unknown" today. There are many poems in it by Ignoto and one poem by Anonimus. At that time, Anonimus did not mean unknown. Anonimus was still a pen name being used by Anthonie Munday.

In the play by satirist John Marston titled Histrio-Mastix', a thinly disguised Munday is called a "peaking pagenter" and parodied as "Post-haste", characterised as a poor actor and playwright who instead of writing and rehearsing, preferred to extemporise and thus undermine the performance. There is a Catholic pamphlet written against Munday saying he did exactly this when young and was hissed off the stage. He was being portrayed by Marston as someone who could dash off a line or page in no time, but it would be awful prose that no educated man could admire.

This caricature of Munday as "Post haste" in Histrio-Mastix is intriguing. The Latin word for spear is hastœ. So, haste, in "Post Haste", maybe a coded reference to Munday and London-Shakespeare being the one person. It is almost the same in construction as the "Shake-scene" reference in Greene's Groats-worth of Witte. Although I believe Shake-scene refers to Edward Alleyn, many people believe it refers to London-Shakespeare. If they accept that, then they must equally accept that Post haste is the same, but points to Munday. It should be remembered that most university men and other well-educated people could read Latin. The vast majority of literate people could not. What may seem to be obscure Latin connections to us, was immediately obvious to learned people in those times.

In the First Folio of 1623, it is stated that the plays are *"Published according to the True Original Copies"*. This has to mean original handwritten copies. Only 35 plays are in the catalogue (contents list) of plays at the front of the First Folio. There are, though, 36 plays printed in it.

There are two possible reasons for this.

The first possibility is that Munday could not find his handwritten, therefore, true original copy of Troilus and Cressida. He may have found a previously printed version and used that. As it was not a True Original Copy, it was not included in the catalogue.

The second possibility is that Troilus & Cressida was stored separately from the other plays and he could not find it. Much later he, perhaps, did locate it, but by then the catalogue page had already been printed. Thus, "Troilus and Cressida" was added to the book late in the actual print run. It is printed well into the second half of the book.

Only the true author would have the desire and the means to preserve all of his own handwritten copies. So Munday, who was 62 years old in 1623, must have had this large collection stored in his own home. It was around this time that Anthony Munday married his second wife, Gillian. They moved out of Cripplegate, which had been his family home for many years, and moved to a house in Moorgate. This moving of house, belongings and years of clutter, may have been what prompted him to finally decide to kill off his Shake-speare pen name. Intrinsic to this decision would be to have his collection of handwritten plays published as a book. Once published, he could dispose of the large pile of handwritten manuscripts, or more likely sell them to be washed clean and sold on.

Stratford-Shakspere had left no written works in his will when he died seven years earlier and not one of his, allegedly, hundreds of handwritten pages have ever turned up. Not in London or Stratford; not even a letter to anyone. If he was literate and did live and work in London, he would have sent dozens to various people in Stratford-upon-Avon over those twenty-plus years.

"And Time dissolves thy **Stratford** *Moniment"* is a line that appears among the dedications after the Droeshout portrait in the First Folio of Shake-speare Plays. This line is in L. Digges dedication to Shake-

speare. Only the word Stratford in this line, as shown above, is not printed in italic, it has, therefore, been highlighted.

It is important to note that the word "moniment" is used rather than monument. Moniment is an obsolete word that had a similar meaning to monument, but it can be any form of remembrance, not only one made of stone. Moniment is not a spelling error, it is also in Ben Jonson's elegy on line 22.

"Thou art a moniment, without a tombe"

So, Jonson, incidentally, is saying that there is no tomb. Not in Stratford-upon-Avon or anywhere else.

Digges poem is yet another simple puzzle, a tease even. The highlighting of keywords continues throughout the poem. To begin with, the poem has the curious feature that W. Shakespeare is spelled in its heading without a hyphen. Then, immediately below it, the first word in the first line of the poem is Shake-fpeare, with a hyphen. Note the medial, non-italic, Long-s.

All of the information in these few paragraphs is read from an original, 1623 First Folio in the Folger library. It will not be confirmed in a later copy off a shelf somewhere. I cannot confirm all of this information with my own 40-plus years-old copy, because it is not a facsimile, the typeface is modern.

My earliest thoughts about the mysterious highlighted word, Stratford, was that Munday was related to one of thirteen Protestant Martyrs. They were burned to death in 1556 by Queen Mary the First (Bloody Mary). Eleven men and two women, one of whom was pregnant, were burned at the stake, together, in the town of Stratford, only seven miles east of London. [Stratford-upon-Avon is over 100 miles NW of London] The victims were not all from Stratford, some were from other towns, including London. This could partly explain Munday's years of work against Catholics, and the story would indeed be a moniment to him. In the Marshall portrait, a disguised "C" and "P", referencing Catholic and Protestant, are on the jerkin chest. They are emblematic of Munday's life.

I now know that this Stratford, is not the real reason for Stratford being in the poem; but I do believe it is the diversional town of Stratford, with its history of Protestant martyrdom, that was in the author's mind when he used the word.

71

We all refer to this book as The First Folio because it does not have a simple title, it has an incomplete description:

Mr. William
SHAKESPEARES
COMEDIES,
HISTORIES, &
TRAGEDIES.

Publifhed according to the True Original Copies.

It does not say plays, poems or stories. What did all the people involved in publishing this book name it when discussing it over many weeks or months? They must have created a short name for it.

'Have you prepared the ink for Mr William Shakespeare's Comedies, Histories and Tragedies, Ed?'

To this day, no one calls it that. The author, publisher and printers would have had to come up with a short working title for it.

It could not have been the First Folio; at that time, every first printing of any folio-sized book was the first folio of that book.

It could not be Munday's book, or Shake-speare's or Marlowe's or Bacon's, because of the obvious confusion with many other printings under those names. Also, it would have revealed the identity of the real author of the works.

The word, Stratford, is a simple code of some kind, in the same way that Droeshout's and Marshall's portraits are picture puzzles, and Ben Jonson's poem, To the Reader, is intentionally devoid of the letters, 'm' and 'y'.

This word, Stratford, is considered by many to be pointing to Stratford-upon-Avon, even though there are more than ten places named Stratford in England. The most likely town it could refer to is the one only seven miles from London. This word stands isolated and alone in L. Digges dedication. That is if L. Digges actually wrote it. This name can be split into "dig and ges", and these two words immediately tempt one to read "L" as Look; look, dig and ges. I believe it to be yet another of Munday's pen names. In Stows two

72

editions of The Survay of London, the name, Digges, is not included. In Munday's 1618 edition, the name is included as a memorial inscription in St Mary Aldermanbury church, Cripplegate. Thus, this name and its obvious pun, being on a tomb, was read and recorded by Munday for his survey. It is unlikely, but it may be true that an L. Digges agreed to put his name to it. But he did not compose it.

We have to consider, why should Stratford point to Stratford-upon-Avon, when the book gives no other information about this, supposed, famous London man? When he died, where he is buried, the family he left behind. There is no mention of Stratford-Shakspere's younger brother, a player/actor in London, who had pre-deceased him. No mention of the famous people who attended his funeral. Nothing about the highlight moments in his London career, nor the, presumed, memorial service that should have been held in London for his many friends? And why, if it's Stratford-Shakspere, did these "friends" then wait seven years to say next to nothing about him? Why did none of these people, nor anyone else, write anything about Stratford-Shakspere when he died seven years previously?

There are differing opinions about this Stratford Moniment line. One is the traditional Stratfordian view. It is that Stratford-Shakspere went to live in London and wrote the works of London-Shakespeare, and so, Stratford Moniment refers to a monument in a Church in Stratford-upon-Avon.

A second opinion, again, points to Stratford-upon-Avon. It is that Stratford-Shakspere was in London, but as an astute businessman, play-broker, and minor actor. He put a variant of his name on the plays because he had bought them, owned all rights to them, and wanted to put his name on them to aggrandise himself. He was, though, not the author of any of them.

A third opinion is, yet again, that it does refer to Stratford-upon-Avon, but as a diversion to direct people away from the true author. The true author could know all about William Shakspere from Stratford-upon-Avon, without him ever having visited London. He could have gleaned the knowledge from William's younger brother, Edmund Shakspere, who we know was a player/actor in London. Edmund did change his name to Shakespeare, presumably for the reflected glory from the plays. He died in 1607 and is buried in, what is now, Southwark Cathedral, a quarter of a mile from The Globe

Theatre. Going to view his gravestone is well worth the pleasant walk before attending a play at the Globe. Edmund Shakespeare's gravestone, in Southwark Cathedral, is the one-and-only Stratford-upon-Avon monument to Elizabethan theatre.

All three opinions above seem to accept that the word, Stratford, has to mean Stratford-Shakspere's home town. This is because no one has put forward any theory as to what else it could possibly mean. You, the reader, is about to discover what "Stratford" really is.

My opinion is that Stratford-Shakspere was never a playwright and had no real connection with London's theatres or plays. I am certain that I have conclusively shown that Anthony Munday is the man hidden in the Droeshout and the Marshall portraits, therefore, he is, doubtless, 'Our Shakespeare'. There is, therefore, no reason at all for Stratford-Shakspere to exist in London, and to be involved with its theatrical scene. As proof of this, we know that he, the person, does not exist in London's theatrical record. Stratford, in the First Folio, cannot refer to Stratford-upon-Avon. It is a reference that, for me, needs an explanation other than being a local family tragedy, or a diversion. It cannot be ignored. The word, Stratford, was an intentional choice, it holds a hidden message.

The Digges elegy poem printed in the First Folio is all in italic except for eight words. They are, Shake-fpeare three times. Then Stratford, Nafo (Naso), Iuliet (Juliet), Romeo and Romans, once each. All except Stratford, clearly refer to people, thus, Stratford is highlighted again. So, are we being told to think of 'Stratford' as a person too? Shake-fpeare, in the poem, is hyphenated, it suggests a hidden author and also emphasises the non-italic, medial Long-s. These eight highlighted words, Shake-fpeare three times, Nafo, Iuliet, Romeo, Romans and Stratford, are telling us something.
The poem is as follows:

TO THE MEMORIE
Of the deceafed Authour Maifter
W. Shakespeare.

Shake-fpeare, *at length thy pious fellowes giue*
The world thy Workes : thy Works, by which, out-liue
Thy Tombe, thy name must : when that stone is rent,
And Time dissolues thy Stratford *Moniment,*
Here we aliue shall view thee still. This Booke,
When Brasse and Marble fade, shall make thee looke
Fresh to all Ages : when posteritie
Shall loath what's new, thinke all is prodegie
That is not Shake-fpeares *; eu'ry Line, each Verse*
Here shall reuiue, redeeme thee from thy Herse.
Nor Fire, nor cankring Age, as Nafo *said,*
Or his, thy wit-fraught Booke shall once inuade.
Nor shall I e're beleeue, or thinke thee dead
(Though mist) vntill our bankrout Stage be sped
(Impossible) with some new straine t' out-do
Passions of Iuliet, *and her* Romeo *;*
Or till I heare a Scene more nobly take,
Then when thy half-Sword parlying Romans *spake.*
Till these, till any of thy Volumes rest
Shall with more fire, more feeling be exprest,
Be sure, our Shake-fpeare, *thou canst neuer dye,*
But crown'd with Lawrell, liue eternally.
L. Digges.

The elegy above is how it was printed in The First Folio of London-Shakespeare Plays in 1623; except that I have:
Underlined the eight non-italic words printed in the poem.
Substituted the unavailable, italic Long-s's in the poem with the modern 's'.
Substituted the unavailable, printers', non-italic Long-s in 'Shake-fpeare' and 'Nafo' with the, almost identical, letter 'f'.

The archaic letter 's' named 'Long-s', resembles this italic *f*, but without the centre cross bar.

Long-s had a non-italic, half-size, printers' version. It sits on the line and is almost the same as this 'f '. I will refer to it as 'flong-s'.

The tiny difference between a flong-s and the letter 'f ', is a deletion of the right-hand side of the centre crossbar. That is all there is that is different, flong-s and 'f ' are, therefore, almost identical in non-italic print. Many words could be confused by this. Would wife mean wise and vice versa? It would be a common and easy misread and could be one reason why both forms of the Long-s fell into disuse.

An important note, I am having to use the letter 'f' to represent both 'f ' and 'flong-s' in these paragraphs, because flong-s is not available on keyboards. The difference between them, as explained above, is tiny. That difference is the same surface area as a full stop/period.

In the Digges poem, 'f ' in Stratford is printed the same as this 'f '. The flong-s is printed in the word Shake-fpeare three times, and once in Nafo.

The 'f ' in Stratford and the flong-s's in Shake-fpeare and Nafo, only appear in the poem in these five non-italic words. They are alluding to something, and so too are the other non-italic words.

"Nafo" is Naso spelled with a flong-s. He is the Roman poet whose usual name is Ovid. His great work was The Metamorphoses. A pointer to what the Digges' elegy is all about.

"Juliet". "*What's in a name?*" A pointer.

"Romeo". "*Wherefore art thou Romeo?*" He is concealed. A pointer.

"Romans". Romulus and Remus, twins. Romulus killed Remus, as the true author is doing to his Shake-speare pen name. A pointer.

All of the pointers in the poem are Italian. This is because Italy is iconic of Munday from his time living there and his, The English Roman Life, book. Yet again, this confirms him as the author.

We have looked, and we have dug, and now all of the above is urging us to take a guess. That guess has to be that the author behind "Look, dig and guess", has deliberately misused 'f' for flong-s in the word "Stratford". We have looked and dug out the pointers that urge us to deliberately misread the one-and-only 'f' in the eight highlighted words, as a flong-s. If we follow this simple switch and read 's' for 'f' in Stratford, then Stratford reveals itself as Stratsord; Straight-sword.

Straight-sword is an obvious alternate form of Shake-speare. Straight instead of Shake, and sword instead of spear. All four syllables begin with the letter S. Straight-sword is a Shake-speare twin. A reflection of the story of the <u>Romans,</u> Romulus and Remus.

As alluded to above, <u>Juliet</u> and <u>Romeo</u> point to another person hiding behind the named one.

<u>Naso</u>/Ovid points to a metamorphosis. We now know that it is Munday discarding his Shake-speare skin.

This obvious alternative to Shake-spear; Strat-sord, will have been the apt by-name used by Munday in publishing circles, and by extension, this printed collection of his plays. It was the name used to talk about it and to refer to the arcane author of it. It will have been used by everyone involved in producing the First Folio of Shake-speare plays.

'Have you prepared the ink for Stratsord's book, Ed?'

Straight-sword, refers to The First Folio of Shake-speare Plays. This collection of plays, in book form, is the Moniment to the hidden author that is being referred to in the line.

"And time dissolves thy Stratsord *moniment"*

The Digges elegy is confirming it's the final curtain for Munday's pen name, William Shake-speare.

Sweet Swan of Avon is a phrase in Ben Jonson's elegy to London-Shakespeare in the First Folio. It does not refer to any of the nine rivers named Avon.

Sweet Swan of Avon! What a site it were
  To see thee in our waters yet appeare,
And make those flights upon the banks of the Thames,
  That so did take Eliza, and our James!

Sweet Swan of Avon was not new, the phrase has roots in Greek literature.

Avon is an ancient British word for river. When we say River Avon, we are actually saying River river. Sweet Swan of Avon is the same as Sweet Swan of River. The Welsh language is based in the ancient British language and the Welsh word for river is, the almost identical, Afon. The letters f and v are almost the same phonetically.

When we read those four lines from the poem, it plainly says that the river it is referring to is the River Thames. It then goes on to say that the Swan of the River is celebrating the river that the monarchs, Queen Elizabeth The First, and King James The First, travelled about their capital on.

It is possible that this is also an allusion to Anthony Munday's London pageants, some of which had floating displays on the Thames.

"And though thou hadst small Latine, and lesse Greeke," is a line in Ben Jonson's elegy, in the First Folio of Shake-speare plays in 1623. The meaning is that London-Shakespeare was not well versed in the classics. This excludes anyone of position or wealth because they would have had a classical education. This was not the first record of this criticism being made.

This same criticism was made circa 1599 by the University Wits – Oxford and Cambridge– in the Parnassus trilogy of satirical plays. This was more than twenty years earlier than the publication of the First Folio. Writers and poets are the targets of the satire, but mainly it is about insulting Munday-Shakespeare.

The plays are about two young men who journey to Mt. Parnassus, the legendary home of Apollo, nymphs and muses. They return in the hope of making their fortune, or a good living at least, and find it difficult.

The only roads they actually travel is the one from school to study at Oxbridge, and then the road to London to seek their fortune. Parnassus is a metaphor for studying the classics at university. Mt. Parnassus is in Greece, but Parnassus, being a metaphor, explains why Greece is not mentioned in the plays. The country that is constantly referred to is Italy. Many of the actors' names, too, are Italianesque. They are listed at the beginning of each play, on Pages 1, 25 and 76, of W. D. Macray's 1886 edition of the Parnassus plays. [It is online]

The plays draw a great deal from Munday's book, The English Roman Life, the story of his journey through France to Italy in 1578. The University Wits have re-imagined Munday's book as a journey through university studies but satirise it and its author throughout. The book and Munday are alluded to many times. 'Reims and Rome', thus France and Italy, are mentioned together many times. They are pointing to Munday. If they were intended to refer to the English Catholic colleges in France and Italy, then these highly educated university wits, were ill-informed and years out-of-date. The original English Catholic College in France was in Douai for many years but was subjected to attacks by Protestants in 1578. The rector, Dr Allen, was forced to move his college 100 miles south to Reims. This may be the reason for the two young men, Munday, with his companion, Nowell, being sent to seek to study there in late 1578. Their secret mission may have been to simply confirm where the Douai college had moved to. The college had left Reims and returned to Douai by 1593. Thus, the references in Parnassus should all be, "Douai and Rome". They aren't, because "Reims and Rome" are a reference to Anthony Munday and his tour through France to Italy, all recorded in his book.

The following are a few examples of pointers to Munday-Shakespeare, read from Macray's book.

Page 5

"The first land we must travel in (as that old hermit told me) is logic" ... *"there are two robbers in this country called genus and species"* ... *"Pacius, in his return from Parnassus had been robbed by these two foresters, but for one Carterus a lustie clubman who defended him..."*

They are talking about their journey through university studies, but are referencing Munday's literary life and travels in doing so. Being robbed on the road is on page 2 of The English Roman Life, page 5 in Parnassus. The beginnings of both of these stories are of being robbed on the road. Munday and Nowell were robbed on the road to Amiens, and Munday says, after they were robbed, they would have been harmed, *"had not a better booty come than we were at that time"*. That *"better booty"* would be a cart of some description. Pacius, in Parnassus, is also saved by a cart; *"Carterus a lustie clubman"*.

The reference to, *"(as that old hermit told me)"* looms very large as, Astrœpho, in Munday's 1580 book, Zelauto, the Fountain of Fame.

Anthony Munday must have been essential reading at Oxbridge because the academic audience is expected to understand the satirical references. They must have known, many dozens of them, that Munday was London-Shakespeare. So, what happened to all the letters telling of this theatrical secret?

Page 12
"Study not these vain arts of Rhetoric, Poetry and Philosophy. There is no sound edifying knowledge in them." These are comments from another fellow undergraduate, not a fellow pilgrim travelling to Greece.

Page 22
This is almost the end of the first play, Pilgrimage to Parnassus. In case the academic audience was still unsure who this play is insulting, Munday's name is mentioned.

Clowne. *This is fine, y-faith! nowe, when they have noe-bodie to leave on the stage, they bring mee up, and, which is worse, tell mee not what I should saye! Gentles, I dare saie youe looke for a fit of mirthe, I'le therfore present unto you a proper newe love-letter of mine to the tune of 'Put on the smock o' Mundaye'...*

This seems to be referencing Munday's extempore acting when young. He was so bad on one occasion that he was hissed off the stage.

The tune was an old, well-known, country dance tune. It is used here as a device to mention Munday's name, in a similar, but not so subtle a way, as Chettle's, seemingly irrelevant, mention of Munday's book in Kind Heart's Dream. This tune was used as a lamentation for criminals for over 200 years (page 156), another pointer to Munday. It alludes to his work as a pursuivant, and at his giving evidence to convict Catholic priests. Then his, decried, journalistic reporting of their executions.

Page 70
A lady has refused to recognise Gullio from his unsigned love letter and he blames his go-between, Ingenioso. Ingenioso tells him that she made him say who sent the letter and that she then replied that the words of the letter were likely not his, except the Latin phrase, because that was written wrong. Gullio (mimicking Munday-Shakespeare) protests at length, finishing with:

"...I woulde prove it upon that carrion of thy witt, that my Lattin was pure Lattin, and such as they speak in Rhems and Padua. Why, it is not the custome in Padua to observe such base ruls as Lilie, Priscian, and such base companions have sett down; wee of the better sorte have a priveledge to create Lattin like Knights, and to saye. Rise up, Sir Phrase...

This satire is supporting what many of us believe. Munday's Shakespeare plays are not entirely his own, many are collaborations. It then says, again, that he has poor Latin. It's that same criticism, and against Munday again; *"Rhems and Padua"*. It is worth noting, it is still France and Italy but not in Rome this time. So, it is not a reference to English Catholic colleges abroad. It points to one man's journey, Anthony Munday's.

This is the second reference to Munday and a love letter in Parnassus, see page 22 above. I have failed to find out how a love letter is connected to Munday.

Page 75
Ingenioso: *Well, fawne the worlde or frowne, my wit the worlde maintaine mee;*
The press shall keepe me from base beggarie

Studioso: *To Rome or Rhems I'le hye, led on by fate,*
Where I well ende my dayes or mende my state.

This exchange is, again, referencing Munday's journey to France and Italy. Then the subsequent publishing, *"The press"*, of his, no doubt, profitable book. *"Rome or Rhems"* again. *"Where I will ende my dayes or mende my state"*. Munday didn't end his days abroad, he returned to England, so, *"Mend my state"* is acknowledging that Munday did well out of his not-so-grand tour of Italy. The Italianesque plays, books, and translations. Then, subsequently, working for Queen Elizabeth's court as a Messenger of her Majesties Chamber. All of this work most certainly did, mend his state.

Page 91
"Flyes have their spleene, each sylly ant his teenes". Ant, as often contracted from Anthony; Ant Munday. Teenes could be tears misspelled, but that does not rhyme as well with spleen. Thus; teenes, referring to Munday being a youth of eighteen-years-old when touring France and Italy, before returning and making a living writing about it.
This may be the earliest reference to the word, "teens", and as we may expect, it comes out of a university.

Page 87
The first two plays vanished for over 200 years. The third play was printed twice in the early 1600s. There are two surviving copies of the third play, copy A and Copy B. Copy A is considered the more accurate of the two. There are many small differences between them and these are pointed out or corrected.

From page 84 to 87, a list of poets is presented and each, in turn, censored in some way and made fun of. Each poet is announced by Ingenioso, then discussed with, or ridiculed by, Judicio. When Shakespeare is announced, it is spelled as "Shatespeare" in copy A. This is claimed to be a miss-spelling because it is "Shakespeare" in copy B; but which one is really correct?

It is obvious that "Shatespeare" was intentional, as it follows the mocking of the other poets. Shatespeare is not contained in a sentence in a paragraph. It is announced to the audience as one word on its own. It is a deliberate, simple, crude put-down to elicit a cheap laugh against Munday-Shakespeare. It is then followed by four lines about Munday-Shakespeare. The first two have been changed to take out the, intended, insults about him.

Original first line: *"Who loves Adonis love or Lucre's rape"*. A question, suggesting they may not be loved.

Changed to: *"Who loves* [not] *Adonis love or Lucrece rape"* A statement saying that everyone we know, loves them.

Original second line: *"His sweeter verse contaynes hart robbing life"*. This is mocking his verses.

Changed to: *"His sweeter verse contaynes hart* [*throbbing line*]*"* This, yet again, sanitises the intended, original ridicule.

We are seeing blind-faith, Stratfordian Bardolatry in action here with these alterations disguised as corrections. It was not an isolated action.

Page 138
The university men's fictional satire has a section where William Kempe is talking to Richard Burbage. The talk is about university men seeking work in the theatres. This exchange is the one most referred to when Parnassus is quoted. As the above, the quote is always sanitised, ignoring the obvious insult to Shake-speare.

Important! This is a fictional satire. It contains a small truth, but it has been amplified by envy of success.

Burbage.
"A little teaching will mend these faults, and it may bee besides they [The university men] *will be able to pen a part."*

Kempe.
"Few of the university men pen plays well, they smell too much of the writer Ovid, and that writer Metamorphosis, and talk too much of Proserpina and Jupiter. Why here's our fellow Shakespeare puts them all down. I and Ben Jonson too. O that Ben Jonson is a pestilent fellow, he brought up Horace giving the poets a pill. But our fellow Shakespeare hath given him a purge that made him bewray his credit.

It begins by saying Kempe is ignorant of the classics.
It then adds that he is also stupid.
It finishes with him retelling some nonsense from Munday-Shakespeare about winning an argument with Jonson.

"...the writer Ovid, and that writer Metamorphosis" This satirical play by the university men, is saying Kempe, Burbage and Shake-speare, are ignorant of classical facts such as Metamorphosis wasn't a writer, it was the long narrative poem by Ovid.

"...and talk too much of Proserpina and Jupiter"

Proserpina's story, with Jupiter, is told in a section of Ovid's poem, The Metamorphosis. The words placed in Kempe's mouth are saying he knows all about Proserpina and Jupiter because the wits *"talk too much"* about them. In spite of all he has (in this fictional satire) heard and been told, he, somehow, has not understood about Ovid and still believes Metamorphosis is the author. These words imply he is stupid as well as uneducated in the classics.

"...he brought up Horace giving the poets (Shake-speare and others) *a pill".*

84

This means that Jonson quoted the Roman poet, Horace. Perhaps, *"Wisdom is not wisdom when it is derived from books alone"* or, more probably, *"Faults are soon copied"*.

"But our fellow Shakespeare hath given him a purge that made him bewray his credit"

Kempe is represented as believing Munday-Shakespeare's talk about winning an argument with Jonson. He has told Kempe his riposte to Jonson's Horace, the purge, was so cutting, it caused Jonson to *"bewray his credit"*, piss his pants. Bewray, means to foul or soil.

The university wits are continuing their satirical theme, Kempe has got it wrong yet again. Munday-Shakespeare was, indeed, the cause of Jonson pissing his pants, but not because of the eloquence of his riposte, it was because the riposte was nonsense. What the wits are clearly portraying, is that Ben Jonson, with others, was uncontrollably laughing at Munday-Shakespeare's ridiculous response to him quoting Horace. The result of this was that Jonson pissed himself laughing at it. The implication [in this satire] is that Munday-Shakespeare was a bullshitter. (*I cannot find a better word*).

A large part of the satirical Parnassus story is following in Anthony Munday's footsteps, following his literary life. Munday's pen-name, Shakespeare, is mentioned several times in the plays. Non-university men, like Munday and his collaborative authors, are successful in writing and performing plays. And at writing books and poems, and making a living from all of this. They were some of the leading lights of the English literary renaissance at that time. This seems to be the root cause of the disdain and satire (taking-the-piss) in the Parnassus plays.

Could Kempe's speech in Parnassus Part Three be the, yet undiscovered, origin of the ubiquitous British phrase, taking-the-piss? This would likely be after 1886, with the first, widely available, publication of all three Parnassus plays in one book. This boosted the knowledge of their existence and importance.

Kempe's words imply Munday-Shakespeare claimed he had shocked Jonson into bewraying himself, and so, had won the argument. Thus, he was claiming his superior wit had caused Jonson's to piss himself. This is nonsensical, and the opposite of what is obviously being alluded to by the university wits. Whatever Munday-Shakespeare said was ridiculous, and this caused Jonson to piss himself laughing. This, then, could have become symbolic of the satire about Jonson's involuntary piss, The Piss. Munday-Shakespeare is aggrandising himself by denying Jonson's hysterical laughter. He is taking vainglorious credit for The Piss. He's taking The Piss.

There is an epigram by Sir John Davies titled "In Mundayum" [57]. It was never published by him but it has survived. It is thought he considered it too cutting to put into print. It implies Munday exaggerated and lied, and was, therefore, a persistent bullshitter.

"Munday I sweare shallbee a holidaye,
If hee forsweare himselfe but once a daye."

Forsweare, in those times, had the meaning of; commit perjury. Thus, the epigram scans easier today if you read 'perjure' for 'forsweare'.

Davis describes Munday as a bullshitter. Parnassus describes Shake-speare as a bullshitter. They are both referencing the same man. Macray's page 70 and 138 quotes from the plays, above, are describing just such a person. As with other references to "Shake-speare" in London. They are actually referencing Anthony Munday's pen name.

The Parnassus plays, then Ben Jonson's elegy, clearly point out London-Shakespeare's ignorance of the classics.

In Tracey Hill's book, Anthony Munday and Civic Culture, she points out, Munday's, ignorance of the classics.

"... and [Munday] *rarely passed up any opportunity to trade on other writers' currency. As a consequence, he did sometimes make mistakes over Greek and Roman mythology that would have provoked the scorn of better-educated contemporaries such as Nashe or Jonson."*

The above references are pointing up the same author's lack of a classical education. It also highlights his reluctance to lose face in discussions.

Perhaps, for Munday, it wasn't about losing face. As a prolific author through and through, it may be that he actually enjoyed arguments and disputes. They would be a source of material and a stress-test of his inventive mind's ability to deny and resolve the undeniable. Could it be that he habitually thought up and assembled stories out of whatever discussion he found himself involved in? If he then, seeking to play devil's advocate, gave voice to them during a discussion, they could be interpreted as lies. How could he have functioned and been successful for six decades if he was a persistent liar? The only solution for me is that, as a high functioning individual at genius level, his thought patterns were far and away beyond our own, personal and emotional, views of the world.

Macbeth
"To-morrow and to-morrow and to-morrow,
Creeps in this petty pace from day to day,
To the last syllable of recorded time;
And all our yesterdays have lighted fools
The way to dusty death. Out, out, brief candle
Life's but a walking shadow, a poor player,
That struts and frets his hour upon the stage,
And then is heard no more. It is a tale
Told by an idiot, full of sound and fury,
Signifying nothing. "

For me, this is near to his mind's workings. He seems to say, manage your gift of life as best you can, but none of it matters. The passage may be his view of life for humans. He does seem to imply that if every human alive today, died peacefully in their beds tonight, what difference would it make?

Munday spoke, wrote and translated Latin, but was not as well versed in the Classics as the university men. He made, or copied others', mistakes. These criticisms of Munday-Shakespeare contain a small truth but they are a hyperbolic running joke. Nashe and Jonson may well have been scornful of Munday's versions of their high art. But the majority of ordinary piper-paying people would neither notice nor care. And there's the rub.

[Note: *Tracey Hill's book does not suggest that Munday was London-Shakespeare*]

There are three other main candidates to be London-Shakespeare. They are The Earl of Oxford, Sir Francis Bacon, and, of course, Stratford-Shakspere. Kind Hearts Dream and the Parnassus plays, being so insulting, means that London-Shakespeare could not be a person of position or rank.

In Munday's book "The English Roman Life" he says that he and Thomas Nowell went to Paris with the two letters from the priest in Amiens. In Paris, they located the residence of the English Ambassador, Sir Amies Paulet, and delivered the letters to him. Before they saw him, they would have been questioned by the ambassadorial assistant, Francis Bacon. Paulet thanked them for the good work and the letters, then gave them money and the advice that they should leave Paris for home very soon. They didn't, they instead spent a few days, or many days in Paris, where they met self-exiled Catholic Englishmen. These men entertained, fed and housed them while persuading them to follow the "true religion". They gave them money and letters of introduction to go to study the priesthood in Rome. Someone must have introduced them to the places that the Catholic Englishmen frequented, if not to the Englishmen themselves. The English Ambassador's assistant, Francis Bacon, would be the most likely conduit. He was only a few months younger than Munday and Nowell, and all three were well educated and spoke Latin. He must have relished the prospect of socialising with English contemporaries for a few days. The perceived links in Bacon's writings to Shake-speare's writings are true. Bacon and Munday met and socialised in Paris in 1578, and it is reasonable to believe that Bacon and Munday became literary friends.

John H. Stotsenburg, in his book, An Impartial Study of the Shakespeare Title, says that he believes, because of their legal allusions, Francis Bacon and/or his brother Anthony, wrote Venus & Adonis, and Lucrecia. Munday-Shakespeare wrote them, but he may have had critical advice and help from the Bacons, or, they could have been full collaborations.

One of Munday's dedications to the Earl of Oxford is in his 1580 book, Zelauto. It is to Edward de Vere, the Earl of Oxford. We know of their relationship because of these dedications and, importantly, that Munday became his servant. That means literary secretary and general literary advisor. Munday would have access to his library and papers. This orphaned son of a printer had reached this position at only nineteen-years-old.

The Epistle Dedicatorie in Zelauto begins as follows:

TO THE RIGHT HONORABLE, HIS
Singular good Lord and Maister, Edward de Vere,
Earle of Oxenford, Viscount Bulbeck, Lord Sand-
Ford, ad of Badelesmere, and Lord high
Chamberlaine of England, Antony
Munday, wisheth all happiness
In this Honorable estate,
And after death eter-
Nall life.

There are then three pages of description of the story mixed with dedication, followed by:

Your Honours moste dutifull
Seruaunt at all assayes.
Antony Munday.

If the Earl of Oxford did contribute anything to the works of Shakespeare, it would be via the man himself, Munday. Some of the reasons for believing that Oxford was London-Shakespeare are actually from his connections to Munday and Munday's writings.

Relegating Munday to a mere conduit for Oxford is digging-through-Troy. The Earl of Oxford wasn't London-Shakespeare, but some of his aristocratic knowledge, ideas and writings, through Munday's genius, could be in some of Munday-Shakespeare's works.

If you lift up to examine the flimsy three-legged stool that is the foundation of the claim that William Shakspere of Stratford-upon-Avon, was the same person who wrote as London-Shakespeare, two of the legs will clatter to the floor.

The three foundational legs are:

First: He had a similar name.

Second: The bust in Holy Trinity Church Stratford-upon-Avon, is of a man with a pen and parchment writing on a thin cushion.

Third: There is an addition to his will, squeezed in between two original lines of the will, leaving money for rings to three London actors.

That is all there is. Everything else is built around these three foundations.

The record shows that the bust had been "repaired" more than once in the 1700s. There exists a drawing by William Dugdale dated around 1634, eighteen years after Stratford-Shakspere's death. It shows the bust without a pen or parchment. The thin cushion is shown in the Dugdale drawing as a bulging sack of wool. The bust probably continued to remain in this original, wool merchant's memorial bust, form, for over a hundred years. The bust is not credible as support for Stratford-Shakspere to be London-Shakespeare.

Stratford-Shakspere's will has an interlined addition leaving money for rings to three London actors. It is undeniably, an afterthought squeezed in between two original lines at a later date. So, was it inserted a month later, or over a hundred years later? Judged against all other evidence, or, rather, the lack of it, plus the fact that the bust was fundamentally altered to support Stratford-Shakspere's claim to fame; logic says that this between-the-lines addition is also a forgery added in the 1700s. In all probability, at the behest of the man who unearthed the will, Joseph Greene. He was the same man who had the bust repaired/altered on two separate occasions.

The Bellot–Mountjoy court case is a curious thing. In 1612, Bellot was suing Mountjoy, his father-in-law, for not paying him the promised dowry after the marriage in 1604. The discussions of marriage and dowries took place in Mountjoy's house in Silver Street, Cripplegate, London. This was a minor civil court case in which a "Willm Shanks" gave evidence and signed as such on the witness statement. He remembers nothing of much help to the case. Inexplicably, the first line of Mr Shanks's deposition, at the top of the page, says he is William Shakespeare from Stratford-upon-Avon and is aged 48 or thereabouts. Mr Shanks's signature is claimed to be one of only six Shakspere signatures known of. It is the only one that, tenuously, has him living in London.

It has been claimed for over 100 years that the signature is "Shaks", an uncalled-for abbreviation of Shakspere, the Stratford Man's real name. There is nothing to explain why Shakspere would choose to abbreviate his name on a legal document. There was plenty of space for the full signature. It is not, of course, an abbreviation because it was not him, it says Shanks.

This misreading of Shanks to be Shaks, seems to have provoked grave errors by a person or persons unknown.

Shanks, is a name of Scottish origin. A Shanks family was one of my childhood neighbours. There are six letters in the Shanks signature and the 'n' is clearly there. The misread mystifies me, it is obvious that there is a large gap left between the 'a' and the 'k' if the letter 'n' was not in there. If you ignore the 'n', then it resembles this: *Sha ks*. The letter 'n' is recognisably between 'a' and 'k', it is plain to see and there is no doubt about it. Mr Shanks signed his surname clearly and fully. So, why would the literate Willm Shanks, sign a document with William Shakespeare as the opening words to his deposition?

The first half of the single sheet deposition is in a different handwriting to the second half. The first hand is small and tightly laid out. The difference is such that about two-thirds of the words are in the first half page. Shanks's signature is at the end, beneath the second half.

The claiming of a Shakespeare connection to Mr Shanks is also because other depositions refer to Shakespeare, even though he is clearly Mr Shanks.

An erstwhile maid, Johane Johnsone, allegedly called him Mr Shakespeare in her deposition, and so too does a Danyell Nycholas in his depositions. In all the documents, his name is mentioned twenty-four times, yet his evidence is uncontroversial and gives no helpful information to the case at all. It is almost as if it was all about Shakespeare, rather than Bellot and Mountjoy.

The relevant part of the deposition of the former maid is as follows:

"*the deft* (defendant Mountjoy) *did send and pswade one Mr Shakespeare that laye in the house to pswade the plt* (Plaintive Bellot) *to the same Marriadge. And more shee cannot depose.*"

These words, "*that laye in the house*" is the basis for claiming that Stratford-Shakspere rented a room, and so lived in Mountjoy's house, in Silver Street, around 1604. It is actually Mr Shanks, and he could be just a regular visiting friend and neighbour, who *laye* comfortably chatting in the parlour that day, and on many other days too. He could be anyone.

It seems from the documents that, whoever he was, he did not want to be involved with this court case. He claims to remember nothing helpful to either side and signed his name as Willm Shanks at the bottom of his witness statement. If the document is to be believed and taken at face value, one wonders why Mr Shanks was called to give evidence in the first place. The case must have been explained to him previously. He had, according to the deposition, moved to Stratford-upon-Avon, so it would all be through lawyers, and he would have declared to the lawyer in Stratford-upon-Avon, that he could no longer remember the details.

The court documents name him as William Shakespeare, but there is no reference at all to him being an actor or a playwright in those documents. So, why would they misspell Shanks, or Shakspere, as Shakespeare on a legal document? This is not a theatrical business document, that is all over with. Whoever Mr Shanks was, he has, allegedly, moved to Stratford-upon-Avon. If it was Stratford-Shakspere, he would use his real name, William Shakspere, as used on legal documents in his home town. The lawyer in Stratford-upon-Avon would know him as Shakspere. It is not believable for legal people to have clumsily misspelled his name as Shakespeare in these legal papers.

The maid, if her statement hasn't been interfered with or fabricated, was the first person recorded as saying 'Shakespeare'. She was illiterate and signed with her mark, an X, so, the spelling of 'Shanks' as 'Shakespeare' did not originate from her? So, why did the spelling of Shanks, or even Shakspere, change to Shakespeare in her deposition? The 1909 claim itself is that the signature is 'Shakspere' contracted. So, where has the spelling 'Shakespeare' magicked itself up from?

The court case took place eight years after the events. Its discovery in the Records Office in 1909, was by two Americans, Dr Charles Wallace and his wife. They had been searching for Shakespeare in the records for years and Dr Wallace claims they had looked at a million documents. It would seem to be good fortune for them after all that effort because the 1612 record was too late to find him living in London. If this, somehow, was their man, he gave his home as Stratford-upon-Avon on this legal document. So, he had already left London and moved one-hundred miles away to Stratford-upon-Avon. As this court case was about monetary greed and gain, one wonders who paid his lawyer's fees. Then the high costs of the eight or more days he spent travelling to London, lodging for many nights, then returning from London. Then, after all of that, to be of no help to anyone in the hearing.

The real William Shakspere died four years later in Stratford-upon-Avon where he had lived all of his life.

The Wallace's did not announce their discovery until the following year, in a minor publication in America.

Their long search had required the Public Record Office's staff to recover every record they requested from storage and to pass it to them. So, they knew everything that the Wallace's had viewed. They were being closely watched and the Wallace's knew this. By delaying their claim-to-fame, they were, inexplicably, risking being elbowed out of being the discoverers of whatever it was they actually found.

Willm Shanks's clear signature, on its own, throws a great, irreconcilable cloud of disbelief over this whole story.

The Shanks signature can be viewed by searching online for Harper's Monthly Magazine. Dr Wallace made his announcement in the March 1910 edition. It includes a photograph of Shanks's deposition with the two handwritings and the signature at the bottom. Even this poor reproduction plainly shows the 'n' in Shanks. A larger signature is on page 33 in the excellent book, "SHAKESPEARE Beyond Doubt?" Edited by John M. Shahan and Alexander Waugh.

Anthony Munday's, The Survay of London, which was published in 1618, would have had advance orders. These would be from the aristocracy, the very rich and the livery companies. After it was printed, each copy would need to be taken to a bookbinder to be bound in whatever material and style the new owner chose. Someone needed to deliver these newly printed books to the purchaser, and then either leave it with them or discuss the binding style, then arrange for the work to be done. With important advance orders, the delivery person would not be the print-works boy. A person of some stature would not only be expected to do it, they no doubt looked on it as an honour. That important person with Munday's Survey of London 1618, would be Anthony Munday himself. He will have hand-delivered perhaps somewhere between four and twenty copies. There is a reasonable and exhilarating chance that some copies of Munday's The Survay of London, published in 1618, were handled by Munday himself, and therefore by London's William Shake-speare. I would conjecture that the pre-ordered copies would be among the most likely to still be with us, as they would have gone to well-loved, well-ordered private libraries.

Munday's, The Survay of London 1633, was still being printed when he died. Although this book is far more impressive than its predecessors, being much larger and illustrated, none of the copies could have been handled by him. It does, though, contain a copy of Anthony Munday's, and therefore, William Shake-speare's, memorial inscription. It is from his tomb within St Stephen's Church,

Coleman Street. The Church no longer exists having been burned to the ground in The Great Fire of London. His ashes are still mixed in the soil under number 36 Coleman Street, in The City of London.

Munday's DNA would, of course, be well rubbed into his extant handwritten works and one-day science may extract it. It may be possible by that time for his face to be reproduced from that DNA and be a near match for the Droeshoute and Marshall portraits. Something of the kind has already been done with the York Gospels. 1000-year-old dust had been collected, then human and animal DNA recovered from it. There is, however, a long way to go, intriguing though.

A Midsummer Day's Dream

There are only two places left in London that are directly associated with Anthony Munday. The first is the church of St Giles, Cripplegate, in the modern Barbican. Munday worshipped there for fifty years and all of his children were christened there. The second is the site of the, now gone, Church of St Stephen on the west side of Coleman Street near the southern end. Anthony Munday, and therefore William Shakespeare, was buried there. There was a café very close by in Coleman Street when I went to pay homage; I sat sipping a cappuccino, grinning inanely while staring at the floor. I'm sure I felt his presence. I don't really believe in imaginary beings of any persuasion, but there was a presence and it seemed to be telling me: 'You've done a piss-poor job of writing my true story'.

Methinks: *'That was the first book, I rushed it out with warts and all, and it does need severe editing. This second book, so far, has no fiction. There is speculation, but not fiction, you, namesake, have the honour of having your own name on both books as the author.'*

Ant Munday: *'Looking at what you have produced, I am not too sure that's such an honour anymore.'*

Me: *'Hang on, let's not be hasty; you are the greatest writer of the times. To do what you did, then, without high education, makes you a genius, you can't expect me to match what you did?'*

AM: *'Not high education? Oh, dear; more research needed. I'm to be surrounded again by tosspots. I think I will refer to you as Chettle -the-younger.'*

Me: *'Tell me stuff, enlighten me, tell me the true story.'*

AM: *'That's your task namesake, dig deeper, read more.'*

Me: *'Who was the dark lady? I have no way of finding that out.'*

AM: *'You're not supposed to invent, stick to the facts and Occam's Razor.'*

Me: *'The facts are 400 years old and vague. There are books out saying Paul McCartney isn't Paul McCartney, and that was only* *a few years ago; some speculation is essential, tell me who it was, give me a chance at a great revelation?'*

AM: *'Paul Who?'*

Me; *'It is said that Paul McCartney, the singer-songwriter, died in 1966 and Billy Shears took his place.'*

AM: *'William Shears! Has history repeated itself?'*

Me: *'Never mind, forget it; tell me who the dark lady was?'*

AM: *'No one would believe you and it would then cloak everything else you have written in disbelief.'*

Me: *'Well it's all true, and people scoffing never bothered you.'*

AM: *'No, it didn't, they were best ignored. The piper-paying people never took any notice of them anyway.'*

Me: *'So, who was she?'*

AM: *'I'm not going to indulge you further.'*

Me: *'I have a thousand questions; you have to answer this one at the very least.'*

AM: *'So, what is it you want to know?'*

Me: *'Who was the dark lady?'*

AM: *'Very well; ET.'*

Me: *'What! She was from another world?'*

AM: *'Kind of, but those are her initials. Go and work it out for yourself.'*

Me: *'That's unrealistic, it was 400 years ago. I can't think of anyone with those initials.'*

AM: *'That's it, your coffee is drunk and your wife is staring at you as if you are drunk.'*

Me: *'She's seen me drunk and knows I'm not.'*

AM: *'Well, she thinks you're triggered and emotional; I do like to keep up with language developments. How did you pull her?'*

Me: *'Charm.'*

AM: *'It must have been an expensive charm; of gold and diamonds was it? Or did you visit a soothsayer for a love charm? You should have asked for a youth potion as well while you were there.'*

Me: *'I'm not as old as you when you slipped your mortal coil. I never, until now, realised that was all you slipped; you are still here in spirit; you didn't let go, did you?'*

AM: *'Well, you sort of fade away in the mists, then, when the last person who ever knew you slips over the edge, that's the time to*

97

go away and become an ancestor in the minds of the breathers. In my case, there was unfinished business, my poems and plays, I regret hiding it so well. I had no idea that a bloody and cruel civil war was less than ten years away, and that everything would change. I can't go until it is put right. I did have a look at you when you were younger when you looked me up in that encyclopaedia. I thought, "Is he going to be the one?" I next saw you at seventeen years old and then I knew. It wasn't going to be you! Why did you wait until you were this old? You could slip the coil and never finish the story. Are you sure you are only my age, you look older?'

Me: *'I'm told I don't look my age.'*

AM: *'Was it a doxy who told you that? I hope you paid her well.'*

Me: *'No, it wasn't. Are you comparing me to your Droeshout and Marshall portraits? You were only fifty-something in those. You shook off the mortal coil at seventy-two. I didn't always look this old. There is the picture I have of me on my three-fifty Matchless in nineteen sixty—*

AM: *'Spare me your histrionics! I remember watching you and thinking, "He's never going anywhere with this, and certainly not on that old motorbike." There have been some brilliant Mundays over the years, and a few of the men were called Anthony, but I could not shift their blind faith in Shakspere. How did it come about that you did, and so late in life? It was a surprise to me: you!'*

Me: *'Thanks for the endorsement; not. I thought you had visited me, put your hand on my shoulder, then flicked book leaves before my eyes. Revealed the Droeshout clues to me.'*

AM: *'No, not me, maybe it was Shakspere feeling guilty; but then he died knowing nothing at all about it, so, why would he? The first I knew was later when you stared intently at the Marshall portrait and saw it all jump out at you. That's what quaked the boards under my stage. I tried to help a little from then on. The urge to snatch the pen from your hand was almost overwhelming, but you don't use a pen, do you?'*

Me: *'Why did you not talk to me then? Why now, when; good, bad or indifferent, I have done the work?'*

AM: *'I can only manifest myself this strongly where my ashes are in Coleman Street and St Giles Church where I worshipped for fifty years. That's all that is left to me.'*

Me: *'So, since we're both here over your ashes, who was the dark lady?'*

AM: *'I am leaving now, but she wasn't dark as in crows, she was dark, as in auburn, now go home and work for longer. And do organise your notations this time. If you do this well, I will be able to take my rest at last. I am relying on you, heaven help me'.*

Me: *'Heaven! Are you saying that there is a God?'*

AM: *'Not as you would understand it, but yes.'*

Me: *'You can't leave something that important unsaid, tell me!'*

AM: *'It's very simple, the only God is Comoh.'*

Me: *'Comoh, Lake Como? In Italy? Do you mean the Pope?'*

AM: *'No, it's an acronym, Combined Mind of Humanity. That's what all gods are. The agreed beliefs, rules and hopes of human beings, and an explanation for the unexplainable; deus ex machina. A little piece of God is inside each breather, even a madman. As for heaven; you, old man, are in heaven now, your life on Earth is it, and you only get one go. If you desire another good life, pass yourself on by having a child and nurturing it.'*

Me: *'Many people have suffered terribly for their Gods.'*

AM: *'God has no physical presence other than love and civilisation. It never hurt anyone, humans do that for their own reasons. Now, I must leave you, you have had your audience, Adie—*

Me: *'Don't go yet, give me more answers? Why the pen name Shakespeare?'*

AM: *'Ah, I will answer that; the sluggardized tosspots used to assuage the guilt about their frugal output by calling me a wanker; so, I used it. It's a pun on onanism: will shake spear.'*

Me: *'That can't be the truth!'*

AM: *'Of course it isn't, dullard; that word didn't exist. I'm well known for my bawdy wit; did you not know? It matters not, I am going now, old fellow, good fortune and Adieu.'*

Me: *'Don't leave yet, tell me more. When did you write the first play? Why was your name a secret? Was your true birth mother, actually—*

99

Mrs M: '*Are you alright! You are muttering to the floor as you do with the television. Do you want another cappuccino?*'
Me: '*Do I look old?*'

Conclusion

We have all been totally misled by a miss-allocation and then a subsequent forgery 300 years ago, two forgeries in fact; the bust in Holy Trinity Church was re-cut to include a pen, paper and a thin cushion as a desktop, then the interlined addition squeezed into Stratford-Shakspere's will, leaving money to three London actors. The following years have not been a great conspiracy; it has simply been a reluctance to dispassionately look at the evidence, and this then led to entrenchment. That entrenchment then led to a massive bias with almost religious overtones for Stratford-Shakspere. George Bernard Shaw named it, Bardolatry. We will never know what has been found in the past and torn up because it pointed in the wrong direction. This includes documents about Anthony Munday, as well as Stratford-Shakspere.

I hope that I have proved to you, the reader, that William Shakespeare was the pen name of Anthony Munday. For me, it is proved by the interpretation of the Droeshout and Marshall portraits alone. Everything else I have then found solidly supports those two pieces of evidence. If you are still reluctant to come that far with us, then I hope that you are now fully aware of the problems and lack of evidence, regarding Stratford-Shakspere's claim to be London-Shakespeare. I am resigned to probably not being here when the truth is universally accepted. There are some wide entrenchments to fill in before everyone can cross over. I have found the easy evidence and laid the foundations. I leave it to others to lay the bricks. The evidence will build up until the truth becomes irresistible and irrefutable to all. Anthony Munday will, one day, be given his laurels back. Let us hope it is well before the quincentenary of his birth in 2060.

Anthony R. Munday. Yorkshire, England.
Armund dot org

The main sources that helped me:

The work of many people over many years, reading, researching, and recording.
Sir Tim Berners-Lee for his wonderful, World Wide Web
The Alexander Text of the Complete Works of Shakespeare
Folger Shakespeare Library
Wikipedia
Wikisource
Oxford DNB
Innumerable university online sites that post their treasures for all of us to enjoy
The English Roman Life. Anthony Munday, Ed. Philip J. Ayres
The English Romayne Lyfe. Anthonie Munday, The Bodley Head Quartos
The Survey of London, 1633. By Anthony Munday
Stow's Survey of London. Routledge edition, 1893
Shakespeare's Unorthodox Biography. By Diana Price
SHAKESPEARE Beyond Doubt? Ed by John M. Shahan & Alexander Waugh
Anthony Mundy, An Elizabethan Man of Letters. By Celeste Turner
Anthony Munday and Civic Culture. By Tracey Hill
Anthony Munday and the Catholics, 1560 – 1633. By Donna B. Hamilton
Shakespeare and Anthony Munday. Online essay by David Womersley
Who Wrote Shakespeare? Online study course, Dr Ros Barber
Sir Thomas More. Anthony Munday and others. Ed. Gabrieli and Melchiori
The Elizabethan Theatre & The book of Sir Thomas More. By Scott McMillin
Shakespeare's Hand in Sir Thomas More. A W Pollard
John a Kent and John a Cumber. Anthony Munday. Ed. J. P. Collier
Zelauto. The Fountaine of Fame. Anthony Munday. Ed. Jack Stillinger.
Who Wrote Shakespeare's Plays? By William D. Rubinstein
The Stage Quarrel. By Roscoe R. Small
Contested Will. Who Wrote Shakespeare? By James Shapiro
The Dark Side of Shakespeare. By W. Ron Hess
Shakespeare and His Betters. By R. C. Churchill
The Downfall of Robert Earl of Huntington. (Robin Hood). By Anthony Munday
The Death of Robert, Earl of Huntington. (Robin Hood). By Anthony Munday
Fidelo and Fortunio, two Italian gentlemen. Anthony Munday. Ed. Percy Simpson
Chruso-Thriambos. Lord Mayor's Pageant 1611. By Anthony Mundy
My mum and dad for giving me my name

Printed in Great Britain
by Amazon

14593057R00068